WHISKEY BOYS

WHISKEY BOYS

AND OTHER MEDITATIONS FROM
THE ABYSS AT THE END OF YOUTH

PHILLIP HURST

To Charlotte,
I'll do all
the work, don't
worry.

Phillip H

BAUHAN PUBLISHING
Peterborough, New Hampshire
2021

ISBN : 978-087233-357-4

Library of Congress Control Number: 2021046286

 Cataloging-in-Publication data is on file at the Library of Congress.

Book design by Sarah Bauhan
Cover Design by Henry James

BAUHAN PUBLISHING LLC
PO BOX 117 PETERBOROUGH NEW HAMPSHIRE 03458
603-567-4430
WWW.BAUHANPUBLISHING.COM
Follow us on Facebook and Twitter – @bauhanpub

Go to our website to see other winners of The Monadnock Essay Collection Prize
and for information on submitting your manuscript to the prize.

For my teachers

≈

One whisky is all right, two is too much, and three is too few.
~Old Highland saying

Civilization begins with distillation.
~Faulkner

CONTENTS

1

BEER QUARTERS

In *John Barleycorn*, Jack London's memoir of his love-hate relationship with alcohol, he writes of getting drunk for the first time at age five, when curiosity got the best of him while toting a pail of beer out to his father who was ploughing a field on a hot day. The predictable result was a very sick little boy, and one who swore off alcohol—a promise that held until he discovered red wine a couple of years later. And though we were born a century apart, and while I can't top London's precocious drinking, I more than sympathize with his soused five-year-old self. After all, I got my first bartending gig at the same tender age.

Back in the eighties, my parents owned and ran a little newspaper in rural Illinois, and my teenaged brothers were put in charge on the Tuesday nights when the *News-Gazette's* husband-and-wife crew toiled past the witching hour to meet the weekly publication deadline. After a hasty dinner, my mother would rinse the dishes while my father glowered at *The Wall Street Journal,* chain-smoked Pall Malls, and delivered fire-and-brimstone hagiographic soliloquies in praise of his hero, Ronald Reagan. Eventually, however, the time would come and they'd gather purse and briefcase, faux-fur coat and sweat-stained fedora, warn me to mind my big brothers, and head back up to the newspaper office.

Approximately ten minutes later, my brothers' buddies and girlfriends would roar up to the house in their smoke-belching beaters, cutting ruts in the lawn and hauling in troves of piss-warm Bud, Miller, and Pabst. My mother's Johnny Mathis LPs would be ripped from the record player and frisbeed across the den, replaced by Iron Maiden and KISS. Beer was iced, shots poured, and the bravest of the brave fired up smokes from my father's ever-present carton of Pall Malls. Finally, everyone would gather around the kitchen table and commence getting illegally, outrageously, borderline eschatologically drunk.

The chief pastime was Beer Quarters, and as with all good drinking games, the gist was simple: bounce coins into cups, loser drinks, everybody quickly gets smashed. As the night wore on, coins bounced and splashed into frothy mugs that in turn were drained, filled, quartered, and drained anew. While a novice compared to my brothers (and although my mug was filled with Coca-Cola),

I'll wager I was the finest shooter in all of the downstate Illinois Kindergarten Beer Quarters circuit. My technique involved standing on a chair to gain the necessary elevation, pinching shut one eye behind my Batman mask, hitching up my utility belt and tossing my cape over one shoulder. Then I'd hold the coin flat between finger and thumb, aiming, measuring, before banging it off the tabletop. As that quarter spun through the smoky air, I'd hold my breath, ready to point at whoever had been picking on me the most and shout, "Chug, asshole!"

But the Caped Crusader's tutelage didn't stop there. For instance, he learned how to properly pour a beer, to roll that precious golden liquid down the glass and raise a perfect inch-thick pillow of foamy head. Other duties included emptying ashtrays, changing the TV channel, fetching potato chips, and—most crucially—keeping a lookout for parents come home early. And while I was an eager enough volunteer, any negligence as to these obligations put me at risk of wet-willies and swirlies and (worst of all) the *marvin*, which is Midwest parlance for the *melvin*, a particularly unpleasant variant of the classic wedgie.

Mostly, though, I spent those Tuesday nights in rapt admiration, watching and learning, mimicking the lingo and absorbing all the best moves. Hence, a kid who grew up well-aware of the boons of fermented beverages. Having witnessed my brothers and their friends get sloshed and rowdy and (despite the zits, mullets, and acid-washed jeans) occasionally even *laid*, the debauchery seemed then—and I must confess, in some ways still does seem—pretty cool.

What all of this ultimately says about me is an open question, I suppose, but if it's true that our lives are irrevocably colored by our earliest experiences, that my experience tended to involve watching barley-breathed vulgarians pound cheap suds and arm-wrestle is simply the hand I was dealt. I cannot change this and probably wouldn't even if I could.

In the decades since, however, this dubious education has proven both useful and dangerous. I suspect it played no small part in my becoming a bartender, for one thing, and it also likely nurtured my Irish proclivities for haunting the opposite side of the oak. But something about the wildness of those Tuesday nights seems also to have imbued in me a hunger for adventure, for new places, new faces, and new experience. A recurring theme in *John Barleycorn* is London's distaste for the laboring life he was born into, hence his attendant flights of travel (always arm-in-arm with his titular adviser), and much as with London's early acquaintance with beer, I can sympathize with that, too. While I didn't trek the Klondike during the Gold Rush or contract malaria in the Marquesas (let alone become world-famous and filthy-rich), over the years I have managed to drink my way across the immensity of the American West and beyond, my impressions fueled and colored by a host of drinks whose flavors reflected both the character of where I found them and the condition in which they found me. To this day, tasting those nectars takes me back, intensely and at once, to those distant locales where I mixed and poured, read and wrote, pined for pretty waitresses and shed the most naïve of my preconceptions.

London points out rightly that a strong head for drink, while a source of pride, can also be a great affliction. As such, sobriety is sometimes necessary (and can even be pleasant in moderation), but to imbibe knowledgeably and well, to develop one's capacity to appreciate this most human and humane of traditions, is a deeply civilizing experience. A push back against the encroachment of the humdrum and an instrument by which to lay claim upon the passing hours. A sign, much like a love of literature and a taste for irony, of having lived an authentic life.

So, I suppose old Jack London has inspired me, from this seat at the end of youth, to look back and try to distill all that bars and booze have meant both to the boy and young man I was, as well as the bookish and writerly middle-aged guy I've somehow become. And yet I find myself both grasping at metaphor and mired up to the liver in paradox: because while our pleasures and consolations tend to go down smoothest on the rocks, so as to linger on the tongue and finish a bit more slowly, it seems inescapable that, abandoned as we find ourselves in this most bewildering and lonesome of worlds, we're doomed to struggle— and absent a string of bestsellers those struggles are apt to be potent, sour, and inveterate—and so perhaps it's best to take life's starker realities neat, with no chaser.

In the end, *John Barleycorn* is a call for temperance and prohibition, but reading it one gets the sense that London is either unduly blaming alcohol for the inevitable hurts and disappointments of growing older or paying unconscious lip service to the social movements prevalent at the time. Because though drink nearly killed him more than once and quite possibly hastened his early death, and though in his youth it frittered away his hard-earned money and led him into trouble, he acknowledges that old John Barleycorn was his guide into the rugged world of manhood to which he aspired—a friend and companion (if a dodgy one) that helped show him the path to what would become an authentically unique American life.

Looking back on his sodden days, London acknowledges the enigma of booze, with its echoes of Classical-era tragedy: the higher drink bears you up, the farther there is to fall; and nothing that feels so good and comes so easy comes without a corresponding price. Then again, much the same could be said about passionate love or big ambition, the harnessing of a great talent or the plumbing of a deep friendship. There is no honest way around these conditions; and like Hank Williams said, nobody gets out of here alive.

While there's undoubtedly much to savor in this life, particularly in the wilder and blissfully dumber days of one's youth, as you get a little older and read a few more books and experience a few more places, you realize there are darker things afoot. This mix of joy and hurt, of optimism and resignation, of warmth and cold, can perhaps be seen as a recipe for the Cocktail of Life. And while we'd all be wise to sip and take our time with that one, to tread carefully and cast our plans deliberately, to measure our words and double-check our assumptions, maybe—as with a round of Beer Quarters—there also comes a time when your best bet is to just close your eyes and chug.

Be that as it may, I like to think the following warrants going a touch more slowly. This is a book, after all, a book about bars and booze, sure, but also about wanderlust and writing, about real people and real places and real problems; and books, at their best, are prisms that can help us make sense of a real life that so rarely ties up its loose ends or makes clear its meaning. So, I've done my best to give these pages nuance and heart, to look beneath the surface and arrange these meditations in a satisfying and illuminating way. If it turns out I wasn't quite up to the task, so it goes, but I do hope you find something worthwhile here.

I know I did.

2

WHISKEY BOYS

Back in 2005, the day after my final law school exams, I packed up my ratty clothing and dog-eared book collection and drove 2,200 miles from Nowheresville, Illinois, to Portland, Oregon, a city where I knew not a soul and had no prospects—a city shrouded by rains that linger between the Coastal and Cascade Ranges like a memory of unkind words, a city so green and soggy it seemed I might sprout roots, commence photosynthesis, and become a shambling mound of ferny ennui. In the months to follow, I bought a waterproof jacket, popped Prozac like Pez, went totally broke and a little crazy, but never quite acclimated to seeing Portlanders sip coffee in the drizzle over moldering copies of *The Oregonian*.

Shortly before last call, on the evening before I was to sit for the Oregon State Bar Exam, a young woman with long dark hair and a husky voice took the stool beside my own. She ordered bourbon neat. Freckles dusted her nose and a gauzy scarf was twined around her throat. Back at her place, she put on some tunes and together we dove headfirst straight down the neck of a bottle of Evan Williams. Although my recollections get a bit hazy at this point, I recall a room aglow with vanilla candles, a TV flickering on mute, and her astraddle me and pushing that dark hair from her face before sparking a spit-dappled joint. A tumbler of Mr. Williams's good whiskey rested on my chest all the while, the rich red liquor trembling along with my heartbeat.

Come dawn, gagging at the foul paste coating my tongue, I bolted upright haunted by a sense of being prone on the tracks, the horn sounding, lights flashing and metal shrieking. I glanced down at the elaborate tattoo on my companion's rump and thigh—a gothic oak tree, leafless and windblown, with a squirrel peeking from a knothole and a raven perched in the skeletal branches. The night before, as I'd sipped bourbon at the witching hour, these images had struck me as quite novel; now, however, with that same bourbon roiling in my gut, the eyes of both animals seemed eerily judgmental. I leapt to my feet and yanked on my stale jeans.

"It's so early . . ." she mumbled into her pillow.

Desperately searching for my shirt, I replied that it most definitely was not early, that it was in fact very late.

"Come back to bed," she told me, and again pushed that luxurious hair out of her eyes, "you big, dumb, sad, lonesome fucker."

Then I dropped into a squat, my knees firing like rabbit guns, and while knotting my sneakers explained I would love nothing more than to crawl back into bed—except I was scheduled to sit for the bar exam. Hearing this, she sat up, blinking. "The what?"

"The bar exam," I said, and jerked my keys from my pocket, "the Oregon State Bar Exam!"

Her hoarse laughter trailed me outside into the drizzle. My old Honda was slung across two spaces, looking like a trail-worn green mule. In the trunk sat a milk crate full of study guides—twelve-hundred dollars' worth of pristine, unused study guides. As I wedged myself into the driver's seat, a wild grimace on my face and the smell of fermented corn leaking from my every pore, those guides seemed as shame-inducing as neglected pets. And while I splashed away through the ashen puddles, the prospect of ever seeing girl, squirrel, or raven again seemed almost as unlikely as a good showing on the day's multiple choice questions, essays, and practical skills testing.

～

Sure enough, a few months later I received a handsome letter printed on 100% cotton, 32-pound, watermarked ivory stationery that expressed the bar examiners sincere regrets at my not having attained the requisite score for licensure.

But I'd merely gotten my just deserts. Consider my approach to my final year of law school. While my classmates were busy job-hunting, bar-prepping, and hastily offering to marry one another, I signed on as night watchman at an industrial park and neglected my coursework in favor of writing a novel. Instead of learning the details of intestacy or pondering the rule against perpetuities, I dreamt up a potboiler. Repressed memory. Murder. Lycanthropy. Fratricide. Sex. And that was just the opening chapter.

In my mind's eye, I'd graduate and then shock everyone by blowing off the bar exam. Soon—perhaps in a matter of months, but certainly no longer than a year—my novel would be published, followed by a shower of accolades. Scribbling away in that stuffy little guard shack, I imagined the book tours, the first-class flights, the sexy author groupies (*were* there author groupies?), and the posh hotels replete with towering bar tabs all comped by my grateful publisher—a venerable Manhattan house whose employees would stand as one to applaud their newest literary wunderkind as he strolled through the sparkling glass doors.

Thusly inspired, I took to washing down my nightly writing sessions with double shots of Ralph Waldo Emerson, having stumbled upon his collected essays in the campus bookstore. One essay in particular—"Self-Reliance"—really stoked my furnace. Especially the parts about nonconformity and trusting in yourself, how societal expectations hamper authentic achievement and how every man has something unique to offer, if only he'll muster the necessary confidence. I underlined so many choice bits that only the unmarked passages stood out. Reading away my nights, it almost seemed Emerson whispered across the centuries to me alone, the great man having penned a strident defense of why *I* should get to be a writer and not have to be a lawyer—"a simple purpose," Emerson concludes, "may be to him as strong as iron necessity is to others!"

Iron necessity? Needless to say, I wasn't much of a security guard. Besides being distracted with literary pursuits, I also began drinking on the job. A classmate (alias Korean Schwarzenegger) visited the guard shack regularly and, along with protein bars and ankle weights, he brought whiskey. Our friendship had cemented the year before over a bottle of Wild Turkey shared during a professional responsibility seminar, sipping at our flasks in the lecture hall's upper deck as the professor droned on about conflicts of interest and attorney-client privilege. But I hadn't really understood the intricacies of the bourbon we drank that day; I just knew it was fun to break the rules. Afterward, though, Korean Schwarzenegger became my whiskey guru. I'd grown up drinking beer on the dirt roads of Central Illinois, and whiskey is basically just distilled beer, so an introduction might not seem necessary—but it was.

Because whiskey is not only a rebellious beverage, but a mysterious, ancient, and potent one. Distillation's history dates back at least to Aristotle, who apparently deduced that pure water could be had by boiling seawater. The process advanced haphazardly until second- or third-century Egyptian alchemists invented the alembic still. Other historians posit the alembic didn't emerge until a few centuries later, but all agree that purifying distillates originated in the Muslim world and then spread west, where the focus shifted from producing medicines and cosmetics to something grander: *aqua vitae,* the water of life.

Distilled spirits underwrote religious ritual and alchemy, the search for the philosopher's stone, lead become gold and life eternal. But whiskey, according to my contemporary guide, was the crown jewel of all such historical trivia. Whiskey of grain and water, of fire and wood, of air and something not unlike magic. Whiskey that hides its charms behind a surly exterior to dissuade the unworthy. Whiskey that—unlike vodka or gin, which cloak their rootlessness with mixers—basks in its provenance and stands proximate of nothing.

"Always open up a dram with a little water," Korean Schwarzenegger said, inserting a straw into a bottle of spring water and stoppering the free end with his fingertip. "And never," he said, as he released a few drops into the waiting whiskey, "mix it with cola."

Instead, he explained that whiskey was a nectar to be savored. A dispensation against troubles and spur for polemical thinking, a muse and balm against the tedious and donkey-like nature of our coursework. The time was nigh, these lessons implied, to leave the Dionysian antics to the ancients and the undergrads and embrace a more Aristotelian appreciation of whiskey's charms.

While I absorbed all of this, Korean Schwarzenegger tutored me in the sweeter wheated bourbons I'd already had some exposure to, before moving on to the less forgiving high ryes. Next, our lessons crossed the Atlantic and he introduced me to venerable blends like Johnnie Walker Black, and then single malt whiskies such as the gentle citrus of Glenmorangie and the dark raisin-fig notes of Macallan. Soon, however, the syllabus included cask-strength bourbons that coated my palate in vanilla and lit my chest like a butane torch, along with peat-smoked Islay drams that confused and assailed the senses—so much so that one evening I ventured to say the latest whiskey[1] we'd sampled, Laphroaig, tasted like nothing so much as a dirty ashtray.

Korean Schwarzenegger grinned, having anticipated my reaction. "Taste it again."

But the vegetal bogginess was overwhelming. I asked how he could possibly enjoy the stuff.

"I remember my first Islay like it was yesterday," he said.

When I suggested this was most likely because the flavor reminded him of fellating the Swamp Thing, he merely shook his head. "Be patient," he advised, in his sphinx-like way. "There's much to learn."

Sure enough, in time I acclimated and found myself enjoying the smokiest whiskies available. And although my budget precluded all but the most infrequent of dabbling with single malts, the deeper lesson was priceless: like any

1 The 'e' in whiskey comes and goes, depending on the region. For simplicity's sake, I'll just keep it.

worthwhile intellectual endeavor, a person only begins to learn about whiskey once they've grasped how very little they actually know.

Luckily, there was plenty of time to study, as my responsibilities as night watchman were negligible. Once an hour, I phoned headquarters to confirm nothing was on fire. To verify I was actually walking my rounds (as opposed to just sitting around drinking in the guard shack), I stuck little keys chained to the walls into a bizarre ten-pound clock that I wore satcheled around my neck à la Public Enemy's Flavor Flav. Otherwise, I was at liberty to read Emerson and write my novel, contemplate whiskey with Korean Schwarzenegger, argue who was the best all-time slam dunk artist (Dr. J, Jordan, or Vince Carter), and eat Domburrinos[2] while pondering how in the world we'd ended up as that most desperately thirsty of creatures: the middling law student.

During our last semester, graduation looming and the pressure mounting, we took to racing management's souped-up golf cart through the labyrinthine buildings at breakneck speeds, startling the rats and spiders and trying our damnedest to crash. One night, after a particularly ambitious whiskey session, I floored the accelerator and took a hard left. We popped up on two wheels and Korean Schwarzenegger was ejected from the cart with a distressed hoot. Amazingly enough, he rolled smack into a bucket of tar water positioned to catch drips from the leaky ceiling. In all the tens of thousands of square feet of warehousing, there was only that one bucket. He was covered in tar. All we lacked were the feathers.

~~~

Along the western frontier in 1794, a group of rowdy Pennsylvania distillers who came to be known as the Whiskey Boys resisted an excise levied by the Continental Congress. The tax, which had been passed in 1791 (and decried and disobeyed by nearly all frontier distillers in the intervening years), was meant to repay debts incurred from the Revolutionary War, as well as fund the newly established federal government. But the Whiskey Boys didn't see this as parcel to their civic duty. After all, following a hard-won independence, what could be more un-American—and reminiscent of the recently vanquished English rule—than a tax imposed from afar by a government the frontiersmen had little to no contact with?

Worse, this despotic tax was on *whiskey*, the water of life, that bartering

---

2 Korean Schwarzenegger's post-workout meal. It involved the simultaneous ordering of an unsliced Domino's pepperoni pizza and a steak burrito from a local taquería. Get a whiskey buzz, wrap burrito in pie, dig in.

currency and blood right of the hardy Scots-Irish settlers. In those times, whiskey was the only practical way farmers could render grains storable and fungible, and thus a working still was a necessity. So, when excisemen began poking their noses into this way of life, they soon found themselves tarred and feathered, whereas those distillers who caved and paid the tax would often find their stills "mended"—i.e., shot full of holes. But the rebellion reached its tipping point when a mob marched on the home of a prominent local tax collector, drank his cellar dry of spirits, and torched his house for good measure.

In response, President Washington raised a militia that rivaled the size of the Continental Army. Although after his presidency ended Washington was to outfit Mount Vernon with copper stills, a malt house and kiln, its own cooperage and a distiller who pumped out 11,000 gallons of rye whiskey a year, *during* his presidency Mr. Washington intended to fund his new government by any means necessary.

In fact, upon passage of the hated whiskey tax, Washington appointed Thomas Marshall collector for the Kentucky district at a salary of $450 a year plus commission. Notably, Marshall himself was a distiller, and—more notable still—his son, John, would in time be named Chief Justice of the United States Supreme Court. The younger Marshall's rulings entrenched the primacy of national over state interest in American constitutional law, a concept we take for granted today but that seemed radical at that time—especially to a species of backwoods moonshiner not long removed from the glen and glade of Scotland and Ireland, the type more apt to burn figures of taxmen in effigy than to pony up arrearages. One has to wonder if the Chief Justice's dedication to the principle of federalism owed, at least in part, to having watched his dad struggle to squeeze taxes from those wayward distillers.

Two centuries later, I came to know both bourbon and Justice Marshall quite well, insofar as my readings of the latter's decisions were often tempered with the very spirit his father helped tax. Nonetheless, I awoke at age twenty-five wanting little to do with the seemingly bright future I'd made for myself. Foremost was an unignorable restlessness. While "Self-Reliance" derides traveling as a fool's paradise, my guard shack reading extended beyond Emerson. *Blue Highways,* a travelogue stumbled upon around the same time, confirmed all my misgivings. The author, William Least Heat-Moon, dumped by his wife and axed from his teaching job, outfits a truck with a cot and hotplate and tours America's shade-tree lanes. "A man who couldn't make things go right," he suggests, "could at least go." Better yet, *On the Road* (another favorite) contains a snippet of conversation where Dean Moriarty says they have to hurry up and go. And yet when Sal Paradise asks where exactly they're headed, Dean replies with a sort of Zen koan: "I don't know but we gotta go."

In my middle-twenties, I remained just naïve enough to take such sentiments to heart. Maybe rootlessness wasn't just for bums, but a galvanization of the soul via ever-changing scenery? Hence my spontaneous move west, as lost and desperate Americans have always gone west, as Sal and Dean went west, as the homesteaders went west on the Oregon Trail, and as those Scots-Irish distillers went west clear back in the eighteenth century—although by the time I loaded up my wagon and set off down I-80, the frontier was difficult to locate among all the McDonald's restaurants, Super 8 motels, and Chevron stations.

While I had no desire to live out of my vehicle or cook on a hotplate, I did need to know what if anything waited out in the world, and to do that I had to revise more than my potboiler novel. The question then: how to rebel when what you're rebelling against isn't imperialist redcoats or federal tax collectors, but (to crib a line from another famed exciseman, the Scottish poet Robert Burns) your own best-laid schemes?

≈

The answer, of course, was whiskey. And having drunk enough of the stuff to successfully tank the bar exam, my well-lubricated sense of irony suggested I might yet parlay all that painstakingly acquired knowledge into a gig as a bar*tender*.

First off, I needed to generate some income. That very morning I'd written checks to cover rent and student loan payments, and then dug the last $2.34 of furred and sticky coinage from the Honda's ashtray. It was literally all I had, and just barely enough for two items from Taco Bell's value menu. Beyond my perilous finances, I'd also thought bartending might leave me time to write, to devote the best of my energy to the page—my vocation—while compartmentalizing work into mere avocation. Most of all, I was simply fed up with always doing what I was *supposed* to do. And that's the long and short of how I ended up interviewing with Gary, the general manager of a log cabin restaurant called the Steelhead Bar & Grill, which overlooked the Clackamas River in the boondocks southeast of Portland.

Seated at back of the dining room, we introduced ourselves and soon began discussing the work experience detailed on the résumé I'd brought along, which rested on the crisp white linen between us. "May I?" Gary asked.

Of course, I replied, and slid the document across the table.

Though hardly the curriculum vitae befitting an attorney, my résumé was printed on the same sort of thick and handsome stationery the bar examiners used to inform me I'd failed their test. Unlike the examiner's letter, however, my résumé listed a string of wholly imaginary restaurants, taverns, and bistros, all conveniently back in the Midwest. Fabricated phone numbers for nonexistent managers lent authenticity, and a string of bullet points enumerated my fictional achievements: *Created seasonal cocktails; Paired varietals with menu; Inventoried and ordered product.* As I'd been busy trumping up this fraud, it wasn't lost on me that I might've actually passed the bar had I studied civil procedure and commercial paper with similar vigor.

"Frankly," Gary said, and set the résumé aside, "you seem overqualified. Our day bartender mostly stocks and preps for dinner. You'll make hourly and tip-outs, but probably won't walk with quite what you're accustomed to."

I thought of my value-menu budget and told him I could tighten the belt a little.

Then Gary asked me about whiskey. In particular, to distinguish bourbon from scotch. I thought of the guard shack and Korean Schwarzenegger and what strange turns this life can take.

"All bourbon is whiskey," I said, for my opening gambit, "but not all whiskey is bourbon. Just like all scotch is whiskey, but not all whiskey is scotch."

Having caught Gary's attention, I followed this up with a succinct rundown of bourbon-making: mash bills of wheat and rye, rickhouses packed with American oak, how Kentucky's sultry summers and icy winters coax bourbon into the barrelwood and squeeze it back out. Turning to scotch, I expounded upon single malts versus blends, sun-ripened barley smoked over peat fires, salt-stung Hebridean Isles and sherry cask finishing, and the clincher: how awakening a dram with a dash of water emancipates flavors and aroma while releasing those elegantly finger-like whorls that (to borrow from yet another former exciseman, the Highland writer Neil Gunn) uncurl in the glass like a lingering benediction.

Gary smiled and tapped my résumé. "That," he said, "was without a doubt the best answer I've heard all day."

All day—how many other desperate bastards had applied for this job?

Then Gary shot me a conspiratorial grin. "You wouldn't believe the jokers I've interviewed. You'd almost think they'd never really bartended before."

I briefly commiserated upon how difficult it must be to find qualified help, but Gary had risen from his chair by then. "Let's get you behind the bar and see you pour," he said.

~

Unlike when Emerson and his friend Horace Greeley ("Go West, young man!") were extolling those quintessentially American virtues, there's no longer any frontier to light out for; and unlike when those eastern distillers crossed over the Appalachians and found a rough but new life, when one crosses the Rockies today it soon becomes clear the West is no longer a refuge for the lost, as it was back in the post-war years when Sal and Dean raced out to Denver and then San Francisco. Instead, Manifest Destiny has swallowed her own tail, and the dream of self-reinvention via geography is just that—a dream.

This doesn't mean rebellion is impossible, though, and it doesn't mean it isn't sometimes necessary. Emerson nails it when he compares society to a joint-stock company in conspiracy against the individuality of its members, with liberty and self-reliance surrendered in the name of a safe conformity. "Nothing is at last sacred," he writes, "but the integrity of your own mind."

Altogether, it seems whatever remains of America's frontier spirit exists solely between the ears of Americans. And while much has been lost by the paving over and franchising of our western dreams, because we've internalized the memory of those dreams—because, like bourbon, they're now inseparable from our native spirit—perhaps like those early distillers we might yet find rebellion and nonconformity in a glass?

But self-reliance also has a more practical aspect. It's about taking care of your own problems, about not caving and asking for help, about seeing things through—perhaps most of all the doomed things that are closest to our hearts. And while I'd bailed on lawyering, I still wanted to be a writer (which falls squarely into that doomed-thing-close-to-the-heart category), but I'd come to suspect that might take a while, which meant I'd need food and rent money in the meantime. Thus, I had to pull a fast one on Gary the restaurant manager.

Once behind the bar, my shoes sank into a hex-cut rubber mat tacky with spilled booze and I did my best to seem like I hadn't just stumbled into foreign territory. But despite much time spent drinking at bars, I'd never actually seen the working side of one. I'd done my due diligence prior to the interview—recipes, techniques, sanitation protocols—but as post-graduate life was teaching me, you can only learn so much from reading.

Gary took a stool and smiled. "A Manhattan, please."

"Excellent choice, sir," I said, and thought: *A Manhattan?*

The speed rail was lined with bottles, few familiar. Bar tools were strewn about: gleaming metal shakers and strainers, twist cutters, jiggers, citrus squeezers, bottle keys, muddle sticks. A red pistol that fired Coca-Cola products and assorted syrups and juices in empty Perrier bottles dated with strips of tape. My knee bumped the rail and a gang of fruit flies rose, torpid from feasting on the sugary cordials: triple sec, crème de cassis, amaretto, Apple Pucker.

So, I knew the Manhattan was a classic cocktail, the sort served in a martini glass although not technically a martini. I was pretty sure it was garnished with a maraschino cherry, as well. Beyond that, nil. With each passing second, Gary's eyes seemed to burrow deeper into me. It occurred to me that, while I'd read a lot of books, I knew precious little about the real world.

Manhattans were brown, at least—that much I was sure of—and brown meant whiskey.

After making a show of unbuttoning and rolling my sleeves and tucking my tie inside my shirt, I rinsed a pint glass under the sink. Plenty of whiskey had gone down my throat, but somehow never in the guise of a Manhattan. Bourbon or scotch? Rye? And what else—Pernod? No, that was a Sazerac. Simple syrup? No, that was an old-fashioned. Or was it cubed sugar in an old-fashioned? The Internet was littered with conflicting recipes and bar-speak. Muddle this, macerate that. And the terminology was confusing: serve up, straight, straight up, neat. Words used so interchangeably they'd lost meaning.

"Classic cocktails are my forte," I said.

"That's great to hear," Gary said, and added that in his experience today's bartenders often weren't well schooled in the basics. "Whiskey cocktails are my go-to," I said. "I mean, what sort of bartender wants to spend his time adulterating vodka?"

"Well, we do offer a number of refreshing vodka-based cocktails," Gary said. He nodded. "Now about that Manhattan."

But I still hadn't touched a single bottle. Hoping to induce Gary to drop a hint, I claimed I liked to experiment with my cocktail recipes a little. Hearing this, he wanted to know just what sort of experiments I was referring to. So, I suggested I might use rye, for instance, instead of bourbon in my Manhattans. Sometimes I even preferred to use scotch.

"But if you make a scotch Manhattan," Gary said, "you haven't made a Manhattan at all."

I agreed with him. Most definitely. No good bartender would do *that*.

"Unless the guest ordered a Rob Roy," he said, and then glanced at his watch.

≈

Although the Whiskey Boys saw their spirits as above the law, society soon quelled their insurrection. Rapid settlement left them surrounded on all sides by other Americans who either paid the tax out of a need for federal support or evaded it by waterborne shipping channels the Pennsylvanians had no access to. So, the Whiskey Boys saw the writing on the rickhouse wall and sent a delegation to President Washington to submit, but—realizing the fledgling republic would fail if roustabouts felt at liberty to disobey tax laws—Washington decided to send his thirteen-thousand-strong militia marching west over the hills and mountains anyway.

As they traveled, these soldiers found the hills deliciously wet with the very spirit that'd caused so much trouble. As one of the militiamen put it, "No sooner does the drum beat in the morning, than up I start, and away to my canteen, where a precious draft of new distilled whiskey animates and revives me."

When the troops finally made Pittsburgh, ground zero of the Whiskey Rebellion, they met no real resistance, and everyone agreed to pay their taxes. Time and circumstance had fought the battle for them and worn down the rebels more surely than musket balls ever could have. A few weeks later, Washington's militia packed up and left, drinking whiskey made from good American corn all throughout the long march home.

≈

Stalling for time, I began telling Gary about the history of the Whiskey Rebellion. But in the middle of my description of how those old tax collectors were tarred and feathered, he interrupted. "I appreciate your enthusiasm for all things whiskey, but keep in mind that when our guests order a cocktail they expect to receive it in a timely manner."

"Of course," I said, and snagged a bottle of Evan Williams. Considering Evan had played a key role in my bombing the bar exam, he seemed a fitting choice for this new endeavor. I upended the bottle and bourbon pooled in the glass. Still unable to recall the balance of the recipe, I pretended the unfamiliar bar was the problem. "And where's she hiding," I mumbled, scanning the alien bottles. "Has to be here somewhere . . ." A frowning look around the back bar suggested the mystery ingredient might be hiding amidst the Aberlour and Remy Martin.

"Did my vermouth order not show up again?" Gary said, studying the rails.

Voilà, vermouth. I quickly located the bottle, but Gary stopped me before I could pour. "That's dry vermouth," he said.

I'd read that vermouth is spurned in today's martini, but *dry* vermouth implied the existence of multiple vermouths, which was news to me.

"There," Gary said, pointing.

Dark liquid, red label. Sure enough: sweet vermouth. A healthy dollop imbued the bourbon with a ruby glow. I topped the glass with a scoop of ice, but before I could sleeve and shake the cocktail (an operation I wasn't feeling terribly confident in), Gary stopped me again.

"Bitters," he said.

"Bitters," I agreed.

I located the Angostura bitters and dribbled some atop the ice. An herbal pungency rose from the mixing liquids. Glass now firmly sleeved, I shook my would-be cocktail hard with both hands—a furious, ice-cracking, ape-like shake—until the metal tin turned painfully cold. Common sense suggested a classy joint like the Steelhead would chill their glassware, and sure enough the freezer contained rows of frosted martini glasses. I plucked one out by the stem and placed it on a cocktail napkin.

Almost there, except the shaker tin had constricted and wouldn't wiggle loose. A good whack against the rail probably would've done the trick but fearing breakage I tapped it with the heel of my palm, working my way around the perimeter, searching for the sweet spot. Finally, tin and pint parted with a satisfying little whoosh of suction.

Now all that remained was to strain the cocktail, garnish, and begin collecting paychecks. I slapped a strainer atop the tin, straightened to my full height, and toothpicked a cherry—but just as I began to pour, Gary stopped me yet again. "Of course, you realize," he said, "being such an experienced bartender, that Manhattans are *stirred,* not shaken?"

Startled, my finger drifted from the strainer and ice and liquor sloshed into the martini glass. As Gary and I watched, the Manhattan wobbled like a basketball slowly circling a hoop. In the end, the centrifugal force was too much, and the glass toppled over and cracked, ruined. As the treacly spill crept toward Gary's hands, he drummed his fingertips on the bar. I blinked to ease the tension but kept my lips cinched. No special pleading here, your honor.

He cocked an eyebrow. "Well?"

"It's like I said before, Gary. Classic cocktails are my forte."

He crossed his arms and savored this absurdity as one might a well-balanced whiskey sour. Then he gave me a look two parts amusement, one part weariness—like a shoulder shrug via the eyes alone. "Believe me," he said, nodding at the spill, "I'd have shown you the door already, but you really do know your whiskey." He rose from the stool. "And you seem desperate enough to stick around for a while."

He was right, too. I did stick around for a while, although in time my desperation lessened. I paid attention and was duly humbled and eventually learned to bartend, to apply all that whiskey knowledge in the real world and thus make a passable living. While in the coming decade I worked bars all over the West, I never bothered with the bar exam again, mostly because I was too busy learning to write, which is a whole other ballgame.

As for Korean Schwarzenegger, he had no bayonet quite as sharp as writing to throw himself upon, and so he ended up practicing law after all. In the years since, whenever we've gotten together to sip a little whiskey, we both complain more or less equally about our jobs. But I don't believe this means our whiskey rebellion failed, or that we caved to society and saw our stills mended. Instead, I think of that time now as a swan song.

We were Whiskey Boys, through and through. Until one day, somehow, we weren't.

3
SGAILC: THE ART OF MAKING POISONS PLEASANT

But it isn't as if a guy can just give up his boyish ways all at once. No, it's a gradual process, and the perspective I'm writing from now—this voice that's speaking on the page, making light of certain things and trying to ferret out the meaning in others—was largely unavailable to me back then, in the anxious and confusing middle slice of my twenties.

For just one example: a sticky conversation that took place between myself and Sara, a fellow employee of the Steelhead Bar & Grill, and one I just so happened to be dating. Chronology-wise, this would've been about seven or eight months after my interview with Gary.

"No," Sara said, shaking her head faintly, "the Bible is *not* just another book."

This had been brewing for a while and, sensing it could be sidestepped no longer ("We really need to talk," was how Sara put it), I'd fortified myself by sneaking a couple whiskies before clocking out. The lubricated tongue, however, while pleasantly numb, isn't always the wisest of tongues.

"Faith is real to me," Sara said, "and it's real to my family, to the people I love. Don't you get that?"

I said of course, sure—but I didn't get it, not really. We were in the mossy woods just past the employee parking area, near a glittering spot that'd later serve as backdrop for a Hollywood blockbuster about lovestruck teenage vampires. Sara sat atop a slab of quarried granite festooned with lichens. On the way, ever the Boy Scout, I'd pit-stopped at my Honda for a fresh bottle of Oban. Now I took a courageous pull, swishing the lush whiskey around my tongue: rich barley, tangerine, a hint of peaty smoke. Korean Schwarzenegger would've surely been proud. I offered Sara the bottle.

"Thanks, but I actually want to feel this."

"To each their own."

"You poison yourself with that stuff so you'll never have to really feel anything. You realize that, right?"

I shrugged and took another drink for the both of us.

~

While there was a dose of truth in Sara's observation, single malt was a spirit I actually did put considerable faith in. Moreover, scotch and agnosticism have something of a history together.

But first, by way of background, consider *A Journey to the Western Islands of Scotland* (1775), which records the travels of Dr. Samuel Johnson while he traipsed the Hebrides with his faithful biographer, James Boswell. Being a Scotsman himself, Boswell couldn't help but have some fluency in the language of his homeland's native spirit, whereas Dr. Johnson was a tea-drinking Englishman who dismissed Scotch whiskey as, "the art of making poison pleasant."

Also of note is a peculiar local term—*sgailc*—which according to MacLeod's dictionary can mean, "a smart knock or blow" (to the head, presumably, as the term also connotes baldness), as well as "a bumper of any spirituous liquor taken before breakfast."

Read together then, these definitions suggest Johnson and Boswell just may have stumbled upon an eighteenth-century Scots Gaelic reference to a practice more modernly known as "the hair of the dog."

In 1776, however, just a year after their travelogue appeared, Boswell paid a visit to another famous writer and Scotsman—the philosopher David Hume. Boswell hadn't called upon his countryman to talk hangover cures, though. Instead, he'd come to Hume on his deathbed, wondering whether the renowned unbeliever—by that point "lean, ghastly, and quite of an earthy appearance"— might like to recant a lifetime of public heresy before it was too late. What were a few quick words of repentance, after all, compared to the soul's writhing in eternal fire?

Whether Boswell had the courtesy to bring along a bottle on this errand is not recorded, but like the deathbed conversion he'd sought, single malt is sometimes "finished" in a second vessel—sherry casks, American oak, wine foudres—and this process can be thought of (assuming one doesn't mind stretching a metaphor) as a last chance to make amends for a spirit's intrinsic faults, to smooth over all those troublesome original sins. Hume was a genuine iconoclast, though, a man who'd spent a lifetime thinking through his rationalism and materialism. So, he ultimately took a pass on Boswell's offer, the reaper on the stoop be damned.

Being a man of devout mind, Boswell was deeply troubled by Hume's nonchalance in the face of mortality. So much so that he later mentioned the incident to his friend and muse, the pious Dr. Johnson (whom Boswell describes as always having had an intense "horrour of death"), but the doctor merely scoffed and claimed Hume only feigned indifference to the New Testament out of intellectual vanity. Nonetheless, Hume's ease in the face of his own imminent dissolution left poor Boswell disturbed for some time—if not even, dare I say, sgailced.

≈

Hoping to forestall the imminent dissolution of our relationship, I again offered Sara the Oban.

While this time she took a polite sip, she was right: the scotch wasn't helping us sort out our differences. We really did care for one another, though. Before we'd even gotten together, there'd been months of lingering eye contact and friendly-flirty banter, Sara posted up by the bar rolling silverware in a stack of green linens while I polished the same three wine glasses over and over. Being so vibrant and pretty, however, Sara had of course been encumbered by a meddlesome boyfriend, whom it'd taken some time to outfox, although outfox him I ultimately did. I distinctly recall the moment the tides turned.

It was a drizzly morning, and I was in the basement gathering bottles to restock when Sara floated down the uneven wooden stairs. There was no reason for her to be in the basement and we both knew it. We looked at one another across the crated beer and wine and I felt again that Sara was someone I might genuinely connect with. She was an artist, a maker of jewelry and paintings who peddled her works at the downtown Saturday Market and spoke of someday attending art school. She was eclectic, something of a tomboy, fun-loving and open-hearted and easy to talk with in a way that's rare—or at least rare for a fundamentally shy person like myself.

Jangling silverware and creaking footsteps echoed down from the dining room. The lunch rush would be upon us any minute, but for now the liquor room was ours alone. We stood just a step apart. I might have kissed her then, despite the boyfriend. There was a moment when it would've been right.

"What's this?" Sara finally asked, her hand rising to my throat. Then she unbuttoned my shirt collar and reached inside, her fingers brushing the skin of my chest. She lifted out the piece of metal I wore on a cord around my neck and studied the mass-produced and characterless jewelry. Then she looked me flush in the face and said, "I can make you a better one."

After she'd gone, I took a deep breath and lifted the stacked boxes of liquor and wine. Hard to see with all those bottles piled under my chin, but I took my time and was almost back upstairs when—daydreaming about that lost kiss—

my foot slipped. I barked my shin and banged into the wall. My attempts to save the leaning tower of booze resulted in a graceless half-turn, a yelp, and a fall. Both cases spilled. Tequila and scotch and a veritable host of wine bottles rained back down the stairs, somersaulting and clattering, breaking and spraying the walls and floor amidst a breathtaking racket.

It wasn't long before another sort of fall occurred, though. But sometimes even that still isn't enough. Because besides matters religious, the months to come revealed other differences. I was still very much interested in writing, for one thing, whereas literature didn't always pique Sara's interest. I wanted to spend more time in the city, to explore the sort of urban landscape my rural Illinois upbringing had left me curious about, and yet Sara was thinking of leasing a cabin in the woods not far from the Steelhead. Did I want to live out there with her? If not, what was I waiting for—for some other girl, a more bookish and intellectual one, to come along? The sum of these differences had, without either of us quite realizing it, sickened our tender relationship.

When Sara began to cry, I plucked the Oban from her hands.

"Please stop," I said, and took another, deeper drink. "I'm sorry."

Her tears flowed so gracefully. That's what I remember best. No hitching breath, no grimacing, no splotchy skin. Just those clean tears gliding down the planes of her face. Unsure what else to say, I offered to start attending church.

"It's not just about going to church," Sara said. "It's about how you feel inside."

Hearing her impassioned tone, it occurred to me that a dayshift bartender with a swollen liver had little hope of competing with the warm bosom of familial approval and the good graces of community, let alone the promise of bodiless immortality. I thought of David Hume and how despite my tendency to play the Doubting Thomas, I probably wouldn't be quite so stoic on my own deathbed. How, in all likelihood, I'd lose my nerve and call out for salvation, spiritual or otherwise—call out, that is, to the very deity who was at that moment looking down in mirth, His having outfoxed *me* to the tune of one lovely girlfriend.

I thought a little sentimentality might smooth things over, a last-ditch jaunt down memory lane. "Remember our first date?"

"Of course, I do," Sara said.

I smiled. "It was pretty trippy, I guess."

"It was more than that," she said. "You know it was."

~

And Sara was right again, as our relationship had been colored by the otherworldly from the very start. That first date took place not long after my clumsy tumble down the stairs. We both had Sunday off and decided to hike the Columbia River Gorge and see some waterfalls. Driving along the winding and picturesque historic highway, the good clean smell of the forest whipped through the cab and a few stray wisps of blonde hair danced around Sara's face. Once parked at the trailhead, however, we both studied the baggie of dirty little mushrooms in her lap.

I asked if they were safe.

"They're from the earth," she said.

Spoken like a true Flower Child. A cook we worked with had mentioned having procured a particularly groovy batch, and while said cook didn't strike me as necessarily trustworthy (all the kitchen guys seemed vaguely criminal), 'shrooming with Sara in the Gorge sounded like a lot of fun. Still, we were both a touch nervous. Such fungi were illegal, after all, though it seems to me now that the criminalization of their magic isn't really about public safety, as the powers that be would have us believe. Instead, it's more about the manner in which they encroach upon the spiritual realm—that sacred trinity that the philosopher-statesman Thomas Paine (who in 1776, the year of Hume's death, would publish *Common Sense* and rally the revolution) aptly christens, "mystery, miracle, and prophecy."

Sara didn't seem overly concerned about any of that, though, and so we gobbled the little suckers and hit the trail.

Half an hour later, passing through a gorgeous stretch of old growth forest, I was sure that cook had swindled us. But then a slight nausea. The feeling worsened, my stomach twisting, but just when it seemed I'd be sick in front of my date, a glorious sweat broke from my every pore and the illness lifted. That, or I was simply distracted by the curious way the cedar chips had begun forming mosaics underfoot . . . which, upon my noticing them, shifted into whorled triskele and sand mandala, before unspooling and coalescing into other, stranger shapes.

I felt unusually present in my skin—a skin no longer of its accustomed seeming, my arms covered in patches of burning red freckles like islands on a map or constellations in the nighttime sky—and it occurred to me that this body of mine was so very strange, not a possession, not a thing I *had* but what I *was* . . . an envelope of flesh that would soon enough sink back into the earth, decaying and wet, like my beloved peat.

Sara hiked up ahead, a halo of light spilling from her limbs and hair. The leaves alongside the path undulated as if undersea, rubbing their mesmeric skins together and whispering secrets in our wake. How could there not be some design in this forest? The sunlight and water, the crunching cinders, the rich smell of earth and all those silent trees trading us breath for precious breath—this couldn't all be accident, could it? Just chemistry, chance, and eons? At that moment, the notion seemed utterly laughable. A ruse, like the voices of birds.

On this point, Thomas Paine notes that the individual who perceives the universe (soberly, he means, in both senses of the word) and yet still believes himself chosen for special significance within it, holds two hopelessly opposed thoughts in his head. Sort of the cosmological equivalent to Keats's famous line about negative capability. And just then—paused mid-step on the trail—I felt mysteriously compelled to announce (not to Sara, but to the enchanted forest itself) that I'd finally grasped Paine's misapprehension.

Sara turned around and asked if I was okay, to which I replied that it seemed possible my thoughts may have somehow gotten spoken aloud . . .

But she just smiled and resumed hiking. Floating along behind her, though, the proof of Paine's error insisted upon itself. I almost had it, the ragged edges of the contradiction or paradox or whatever it was. But then the mountainous impossibility of such thoughts buried me in uncertainties and doubts and I realized I'd been staring down at my feet for an awfully long time, admiring their ridiculous size and flipper-like evolution—until a sound from the trail ahead yanked me back to what passed for reality. Not the chorus of birds or susurrus leaves but gathering menace: a quaking sense of imminent predation, of impending doom.

I'd just begun to wonder if I'd perhaps poisoned myself with one too many magical mushrooms, when the hominid rounded a bend and loped straight at me. A Sasquatchian grotesque, nude or skinned or worse, it thundered down the trail on bristly knees, hands swinging like meathooks, its face twisted into a panting grimace of spittle-flecked incisors.

Woebegone, lost, I flung myself into a bed of ferns.

But then Sara was there, rubbing me down like a spooked horse. *Trail runner,* she kept saying, *Just a trail runner,* until we both succumbed to a bout of mad giggles.

Later, we reached trail's end. In the way of waterfalls, one led to the next and we followed a tumbling creek deep into the forest. Immaculate light lanced the canyon walls and a towering silence rose around us, much as the gothic cedars rose over the water—water that slipped over the mossy shelf to tumble and break in a ghostly spray upon boulders like the skulls of whales. Without a word, Sara stepped into the glacial stream. Up past her boots and near the edge she went, daring the slick bed and the falls. She glanced back at where I sat upon a red log gone soft in the forest's humid palm, and then in one graceful motion she peeled down her shorts and squatted. It was that oldest of human poses, African and primordial, her golden hair spilling down to the globes of her bare rump like a vision for the trail to Damascus. In the rich sunlight, her urine coruscated with all the brilliance of stained glass, braiding with the snowmelt and washing over the falls on its way to the Columbia and finally the Pacific. Then she rose and beckoned me to her, and I couldn't help but gasp when the icy waters baptized my naked and bug-bitten ankles.

~

"Sara, I'm sorry, but don't you ever think maybe all that stuff is just . . ."

The piece of jewelry she'd made for me—a dab of pewter and sliver of shell on a cord—knocked gently against the divot in my throat.

"Just what?"

Our conversation had only gotten worse; that is, gotten closer to the sort of troublesome honesty you can't ever really come back from.

"Never mind, I—"

"No, say what you actually mean for once."

Again, it was her tone, or something beneath her tone, an implication of uncertainty or even cowardice on my part, which (along with too much Oban) finally pushed me over the slippery edge. Sara wasn't trying to save me, I don't think; hers wasn't the patronizing attitude James Boswell took with David Hume, and yet she nonetheless spoke with a certainty I couldn't grasp. I understood that she'd armored herself against the unknowable in a fashion not so altogether different from my drinking and reading, but how could anyone be so sure of a future state, of mystery and miracle and prophecy?

More to the point, how do two peoples' beliefs about the unearthly and unprovable come to poison their here and now? What was the good of agnosticism, after all—let alone books written by guys like Hume and Thomas Paine, which tend to leave the reader with little choice *but* agnosticism—if the unbeliever still finds himself bereft of answers and with no way of circumventing the various dogma, religious or otherwise, that hamstring one's chances for tranquility in a godless world brimming over with godly friends and lovers?

Sick with frustration and already dreading the return of the old loneliness, I heard my voice as if coming from another's throat, using phrases like *wish-thinking* and *spiritual gobbledygook* and calmly but insistently peppering Sara with questions we both knew she couldn't answer, because they were the sort of questions human beings aren't meant to answer, which is to say I was being immature and unfair at best, if not flatly cruel—although to *whom* that cruelty was actually directed now feels a bit harder to say.

In the silence to follow, Sara hopped down from the slab of granite and the hurt and raw look on her face had me backtracking and claiming I'd misspoken, that I hadn't meant those things the way they'd sounded, that I was awfully damn sorry, that it was just the whiskey talking.

When still she didn't speak, I dropped the Oban in the weeds, took her face in my hands and kissed her. Our first kiss had been magical—in a 'shroomy sort of way and a lovestruck Hollywood sort of way—but much like the sequels to those teenybopper vampire flicks, this last kiss felt strained. And Sara apparently felt the same way, because after the briefest taste of salt and whiskey on her plump bottom lip, she recoiled from my smoky breath and looked at me in shock—almost as if (instead of rakish fangs) I'd sprung a pair of horns and a pointy red tail.

Then she spun on the heels of her nonslip shoes and walked away.

From that greenly eerie pocket in the trees behind the restaurant, I heard her old primer gray Chevy cough to life. Then tires spitting gravel. Between my feet lay the bottle, that trustiest of companions, my very own private Boswell. But upon kneeling to retrieve it, I grimaced against a sudden ache in my skull—a bolt of pain just behind the eyes in that mysterious place where one sometimes almost cannot help but feel as if the soul must reside.

4

HODADS IN WONDERLAND

"OB," read the sign at The Tilted Stick, "WHERE THE DEBRIS MEETS THE SEA."

The Stick was a dingy pool hall catty-corner from my new apartment, the sort of place where come last call drunk and lonely guys fought like stray dogs, howling and bleeding in the spilled beer; while "OB" stood for Ocean Beach, the SoCal surfing community where I washed up at age twenty-seven, lost and alone and without the requisite surfboard.

Freshly (and justly) dumped by Sara up in the Portland, and still reeling from having dumped my law career back in Illinois, I'd rather impulsively tossed my books and papers into the Honda yet again, doped my trusty black tomcat, Bart, with tranquilizers, and boogied south down I-5. A few days later, I followed an exit toward the Pacific, where the road petered-out near the San Diego River estuary amidst rotting kelp, empty beer cans, and a glut of cheap-but-tasty burrito shacks. I leased the first apartment I saw, filled it with a couple hundred bucks worth of Craigslist furniture (after delousing the upholstery), and bought a pair of sky-blue board shorts from the surf shop across the street.

In many ways, at least to my Midwestern eyes, OB seemed the prototypical beach community. Restaurants served fish tacos and oysters on the half-shell, the low-slung bungalows and moldy sea-scoured apartment buildings were populated almost exclusively by young singles, radio hits from Sublime and Red Hot Chili Peppers blared from the open-air bars, Chargers flags hung from the streetside balconies, and there was absolutely nowhere to park. But unlike the rest of San Diego's coastal haunts, OB had managed to retain a sense of its past.

In the early twentieth century, the beach was home to a vast amusement park called Wonderland. In fact, my new apartment sat at the very intersection that in 1913 had constituted the park's entrance—and a spectacular entrance it was, framed by towering minarets and lit by thousands of Tungsten lights. Visitors to Wonderland were greeted by a skating rink and dancing pavilion, Japanese tea gardens, a carousel and waterslide, as well as the Blue Streak Racer, the largest rollercoaster on the Pacific seaboard. The park also contained a menagerie of exotic animals, including bears, lions, wolves, monkeys, and one presumably lonely hyena.

The community I would come to know still felt part this carnival history. Feral parrots squawked in the palms just beyond my bedroom window, and festive but shady characters tromped up and down the stairs at all hours of the day and night, as my neighbors were well-known purveyors of weed and coke. Longhaired dudes shot down the street on their longboards, leash-towed by slobbery pit bulls, and there was a homeless woman with a voice like Tommy Lee Jones who crashed on my porch whenever it rained, only to leave behind a tidy pile of cigarette butts, a neat line of empty airplane-sized vodka shooters, and a single plucked tulip.

I didn't really mind the grunginess, though. Yes, the police helicopter (the "ghetto bird") had a tendency to hover over my apartment building at three a.m., searchlight swinging from alleyway to alleyway; and, sure, there were dirty needles in the sand, but come sunset that same sand glowed with a heartbreaking palette of oranges and pinks and blues. In such lights and at such moments, beach and buildings seemed imbued with a doomed romanticism, as if about to slip off the edge of the continent and sink beneath the silvery waves, like a new Atlantis.

The locals, too, had retained something of Wonderland's aura. Everyone was on wheels—skateboards, rollerblades, banana-seat beach cruisers—an entire community of castoffs and layabouts zooming past my front porch, drunk on the golden sunshine and stoned on a beachy serenity. The older and raspier OBecians, refugees from the sixties by and large, had a ghostly vibe, like they might've *always* been there rolling joints and squinting into the mist, while the younger ones ran the gamut from the merely eccentric to the downright bizarre.

There were assorted street performers with their card tricks and handstands and llamas, and Steinbeckian homeless dudes jollily brown-sacking their liquor while strumming and drumming for change. Come the weekend, puffed-up jarheads from Camp Pendleton would roll through, looking to pound drinks and start fights and get—if not laid—at least tattooed.

Speaking of, a neighbor of mine could've rightly been confused with Bradbury's Illustrated Man, as every inch of his flesh, from the crown of his shaven scalp down to his toes, was covered in scrolling reds and greens and gray. The first time I endeavored to say hello to this extraordinary-looking individual, he paused on the sidewalk and blinked at me long and slow, revealing a pair of eerily realistic eyeballs inked on the backs of his lids. "I require nothing . . ." he said, in a robotic monotone—and what could I do but take him at his word?

Then there was Bagman Jehovah, a local keyboardist who sang lugubrious gospel dirges along the tourist thoroughfare. An ancient black man, tall and skinny and bent, he dressed in layers of flowing cloaks and skirts despite the never-ending summer. His gospels somehow captured the essence of sea and indigo sky, the laidback *joie de vivre* of my neighbors, the surfers who'd discovered a new religion at morning tide and the bevies of bikini-clad young women doing pretty things with water and sunshine. Listening to Bagman testify while perched on a barstool overlooking the Pacific, a guy could almost believe in that god he so elegantly praised. More than once, I wished Sara was there to hear him.

But Sara wasn't there, and neither was anyone else I knew. And yet I wasn't necessarily lonely. There was too much to see and take in for that. Because despite my being surely the most uncool character in all of Ocean Beach—my Irish skin freckled instead of tanned, my haircuts cost twelve bucks, and my wardrobe might've been best described as "Midwest-dork"—I found myself totally fascinated. OB seemed to exist outside the normal constraints of place and time, and thus many a day was lost at the rail of one bar or another, watching the froth and flotsam roll in while draining longnecks and allowing the hours to slide off my skin like a film of sweat. Only a decade later did I understand I wasn't merely savoring a mid-twenties cocktail of vitamin D, booze, and lack of responsibility. Instead, for the first time, I'd found a place where I might actually fit in—although this wasn't necessarily apparent at first glance.

Consider a day shortly after the move. It wasn't quite noon yet, but I'd posted up on the streetside patio of a bar called the Sunshine Company. I was delving into my second pint when I noticed a line forming outside a restaurant down the block. The sign painted on the curbside wall read "Hodad's" and featured a toucan-nosed little fellow astraddle the topside bun of a giant hamburger with humanoid arms and legs. This hamburgerman had just caught a wave on his bright red surfboard.

I turned to the guy at the next table over, who was nursing a pint of his own. "Those burgers must be pretty good for the line to wrap around the block like that."

At first, he ignored me. His face was sunburned, the ridge of his nose peeling in white flakes like fish scales. He wore the standard OB uniform of reflective shades and a flat-billed cap, shin-length Dickies, and a black T-shirt. "Hodad's is dank, bro," he finally said.

I squeezed a wedge of lime into my beer. "What is a hodad, anyway?"

Then, after a dismissive smirk at the pale legs sticking out of my newly purchased board shorts, he turned his weathered face once more to the Pacific swelling and breaking down at the blue and gull-hung end of Newport Avenue. "A hodad," he explained, "is somebody who lives in a surfing community but doesn't surf."

~

A poseur, in other words. A wannabe. Or in my case, maybe just a misfit.

Regardless, I had little interest in riding the waves. My left knee was wrecked from a youthful and lopsided love affair with basketball, and the water in Southern California is cold and rough. No, the pull I felt in Ocean Beach owed not so much to the tides, but to the sort of people the place attracted, as if the West Coast were a drain siphoning off refugees from mainstream America. An enclave. A home for oddballs and outcasts and exiles.

Even a self-proclaimed exile needs a job, though, and I couldn't seem to land one in OB. A week or so later, however, I scored an interview in Hillcrest, another San Diego neighborhood that might also be described as populated with outsiders—although on the day of my interview, I didn't know Hillcrest from any other place.

I sat talking with Casa de Agave's owners, Jim and Juan Antonio, at an *azul*-tiled table on the recessed patio. Hanging plants and tasteful brass lanterns cordoned off a bustling University Avenue. A young waiter with a golden tan and a skin-tight polo served us iced tea with lemon. Jim thanked the waiter, who then batted his handsome lashes and drifted away.

Jim and Juan Antonio were partners, they said—*business* partners—and La Cantina, the renovated bar, opened in a week. They needed a bartender who knew tequila and felt comfortable serving upscale clientele.

"Your résumé stood out," Jim said, "because we saw you have a Juris Doctorate."

"Past life," I said.

"I was in law enforcement before becoming a restaurateur," Jim said. "I've always admired the work of prosecuting attorneys."

Then I happened to glance down the block, where a dozen rainbow flags fluttered proudly outside a bar called Urban Mo's. This bar overflowed with men in colorful tank-tops. One of these men, I was fairly certain, wore a cheetah costume. Another was a pink elephant with a conspicuously placed trunk. All seemed to be having a really good time. Music thumped and drinks flowed.

Ah, I thought, *I see.*

"So, please tell me, Phillip," Juan Antonio said, speaking with the overly precise diction of one who conducts business in a foreign language, "why is it that you do not practice law?"

Although I really shouldn't have been caught off-guard by the question, I was. So, I faced my prospective employers and mumbled something vague about writing a novel.

"How interesting," Jim said. "A lawyer *and* a writer."

Then he made a point of explaining that at least half of Casa de Agave's clientele were gay and lesbian . . . with the silence to follow meant to assess whether I was comfortable with that—whether, that is, I wasn't some sort of peripatetic bigot who'd wandered his way down to San Diego only to ignorantly apply for work in the festive heart of the gay district.

I can't recall exactly how I answered Jim's question, but whatever I said must've assuaged his concerns, because the next day he called to offer me the job. And so there I found myself, doubly the hodad: a guy living in a surfing community who did not surf, and a bartender working in a gay community who was not gay.

≈

Originally, Wonderland was envisioned as family-friendly (the dance floor allowed neither "turkey-trotting" nor "bunny-hugging"), but the OB I discovered fell a tad short of such moral sanitation. The Haight-Ashbury of San Diego, it'd traded lions and rollercoasters for tattoo parlors and head shops. In fact, instead of Wonderland, modern OB often seemed more like Neverland—except the Lost Boys were all in their mid-thirties and Tinker Bell sprinkled not pixie, but angel dust.

This is not to say I was anything less than enchanted, though. California is named after an imaginary island in a long-lost Spanish romance, and OB felt similarly make-believe. Street kids wandered through the farmer's market amidst the aromas of kettle corn and frying food, peacock feathers poking from their matted hair and books about LSD and the American Dream quivering in their unwashed hands, while adventuresome foreigners dangled from the steps of the local youth hostel, their dreadlocks as frayed as the rope circling the pilings down along the pier. People not so unlike myself, really, in search of whatever vestige of Wonderland's uniqueness had survived the commodification of drug culture and skyrocketing rents, like the last sweet drops from a steamed agave.

Growing up in rural Illinois, amidst conservative Christians and familial expectations and that practical and soul-molding geometry of corn and bean fields, I'd not even realized a place like OB *could* exist.

And then there was Casa de Agave.

The place drew a mixed crowd of just the sort of young urbans who make for the best clientele. The vibe was peaceful, the food terrific, there were no televisions blaring ESPN, and no detail had been overlooked—the concrete floor was stylishly distressed, the ceiling overlain with repurposed sandalwood, the fireplace hedged with intricate turquoise tiling, the tables set with a hotchpotch of tasteful Baja crockery, and soft California sunshine poured down from the skylights as orange and rich as if filtered through a bottle of Grand Marnier.

The bar itself was intimate, a dozen seats horseshoed around a well from which I mixed a thoughtfully curated list of Latin-themed cocktails. Between the pleasant atmosphere and tasty drinks, Casa de Agave drew a thick crowd. On the busiest nights, it was as if I were the hub on a wheel of thirsty bar-goers, mixing and pouring so fast that the room began to tilt and spin like one of Lowry's soul-displacing benders from *Under the Volcano*. The place was a lot of fun, though. Back in the Midwest, people tended to treat their nights out like coldblooded business exchanges, to glare at their well-meaning bartender as one might a particularly slimy used car salesman, whereas the party in San Diego ebbed and flowed like the sun-dappled waves of the Pacific. Ultimately, however, what made Casa de Agave truly special was the people.

Consider a pair of regulars, Arturo and Bentley, both of whom showed up my very first night working the renovated cantina. Arturo was a lawyer, which provided us a common ground for commiseration ("You dodged a bullet, dude," he'd often say). Rumor had it he'd begun frequenting the restaurant while dating the coquettish waiter who'd served iced tea during my interview. Even though that relationship hadn't lasted, Arturo loved Casa de Agave and always treated the staff with great respect and deference, as if secretly afraid of being rejected.

As for Bentley, he held a PhD in physics and was vice-president of a local software firm. He drank only red wine (despite being in a tequila bar) and drove a Porsche in spite of the fact that he and his siblings (Mercedes and Aston) were all named after luxury cars by their hardworking Chinese immigrant father.

These two men sat opposite each other, Arturo slurping a dirty martini as Bentley nursed a glass of cabernet that he'd swirled, nosed, and subsequently declared middling at best.

"I detect notes of wet stone," I said, a descriptor that seemed foodie enough (and pretentious enough) to pass muster, "and dark, ripe figs."

"Do you now?" Bentley said. "Because I detect Safeway."

Although our wine list was a work-in-progress, Casa de Agave was busy owing to a glowing write-up in the *Union-Tribune*. Thirsty people streamed in faster than the hostess could seat them and the bar was swamped in drink tickets: Coronas, Dos Equis, caipirinhas, mojitos, pomegranate margaritas, sangrias, and chilled shots of Don Julio Blanco. I mixed more drinks over a single weekend than in a month back at the Steelhead.

"Why did you move to California?" Bentley asked.

I glanced up, my hands mechanically dancing: glass, scoop, ice, liquor, mixer, garnish, ticket, glass, scoop, ice, liquor . . . "Got sick of the rain, I guess."

"You live here in the gayborhood?"

When I told him I lived in Ocean Beach, he wrinkled his nose and explained how San Diego's beach communities—Pacific Beach, Mission Beach, and Ocean Beach—were known by their initials: PB, MB, and OB. "Partly Bums," he said, "Mostly Bums, and *Only* Bums."

"OB is growing on me," I said.

"Like a genital wart?"

"Oh, come on. It's not that bad."

"Fine, I suppose Hillcrest and OB can get along. So, you must be a surfer?"

I recalled that conversation from the Sunshine Company. "Nope, never even tried it."

Then Bentley asked if I lived alone. After rimming two glasses with lime and salt, I necked tequila and triple sec between the fingers of each hand and upturned all four bottles at once. A dash of homemade sour and a harried server stabbed the ticket and disappeared with the fresh drinks. Finally, I told Bentley I had a roommate.

He sipped his wine. "Roommate, or partner?"

When I admitted that my roommate was actually a potbellied little tomcat, Bentley sucked his purple teeth and leaned over the bar. "Tell me," he said, "are you in the family?"

"The family?"

"Don't play dumb. You know what I mean."

I confessed then that I was not actually in the family but assured him I was still a pretty good bartender, to which he replied that he'd seen better but would tip anyway. In the meantime, Arturo's cocktail was empty yet again. His eyes were glassy, tie loose, suit wrinkled. "Good cocktails," he said, "are the only things that make this godawful planet bearable."

I mixed him another (very dirty, very watery) and placed it on a fresh napkin.

"How can you drink those?" Bentley asked from across the bar.

Arturo swayed on his stool. "Are you speaking to me?"

"Dirty martinis?" Bentley pursed his lips. "Do you actually *enjoy* the taste of seawater?"

"Dude," Arturo said to me, "Jim and Juan Antonio tell me you're a writer."

Bentley huffed and said he wanted to read it, whatever it was.

Arturo drained his glass in two gulps. "I just finished *Laughter in the Dark*," he said. "It's so real, so true. Nabokov understands, dude. He knows that life is a slog, that love always goes unrequited, and that we're all *fucked*. He knows the bombs are gonna fall—"

"I've always enjoyed Neil Gaiman," Bentley said, pronouncing the author's name with salty lewdness. "He's a fantasy author, you know. The type who imagines the wildest things . . ."

I faced Arturo. "I haven't read much Nabokov, but—"

"And Truman Capote"—Bentley swirled his wine, widened his purple grin— "I heard he wrote while naked on a hotel bed with his tush in the air."

"Dude!" Arturo said, halfway up from his stool. He seemed to expect me to bounce Bentley from La Cantina, but I was far too busy to mediate. Hunkered over the well, my knee howling, I washed down a few Advil with a botched margarita and did my best to keep up with the flood of drink tickets. Hours later, bone-tired and feet numb as stones, I jammed a lime down the neck of an icy Pacifico and settled the night's receipts, only to see that Bentley had tipped twenty on his sixteen-dollar tab, while Arturo tipped forty on thirty.

~

I met Kelly and Shane at a Newport Avenue dive called Pacific Shores.

The three of us had gotten to talking about whatever twentysomething strangers talk about at one a.m. in dark, dank little bars, and it was eventually determined a nightcap was in order. I suspect now this was more Kelly's idea than Shane's, but he was the type to just go with the flow. Sprawled on my ratty couches with a bottle of Hornitos on the coffee table, they told me how they'd come to live in OB.

Shane had grown up in the Oklahoma Bible Belt where his father made a lot of money in natural gas. Then his father had a heart attack. His mother remarried a week or two after Shane graduated from high school. And so Shane found himself a kid with a healthy trust fund, but with no real family and nowhere to go.

"I wasted a decade drunk in Houston," he said. He explained that college hadn't worked out, neither had his various jobs, and his mother seemingly forgot all about him. With nothing much left to lose, he hit the road. After stops in New Orleans and Atlanta, Shane met a girl.

"We got tats together," he said, and then rolled up his pant leg to reveal Puff the Magic Dragon on his plump calf.

Shane's girlfriend was into the music scene, though, and so they'd eventually moved out to L.A., where Shane had quickly fallen into a depression and his girlfriend just as quickly fell for a fellow musician.

"What a bitch," Kelly said.

I liked her curly brown hair, the mischievous way it bounced in her eyes.

"Don't say that, Kel," Shane said. "She just got lonesome, you know? And if she hadn't dumped my ass I never would've found OB."

Then Kelly told her story. Like me, she'd grown up in the Midwest, having graduated from the University of Wisconsin as a literature major. "At some point, I realized I'd spent four years and thirty grand getting a degree in reading books," she said. "I couldn't see myself as a teacher, and no other job paid half as much as I made waiting tables in the same shitty bars where I'd hung out back in college."

From the corner of my eye, I noticed Shane inspecting the shadowy crevice between my Craigslist couches.

"Eventually," Kelly said, "I got sick of my parents ragging on me for not using my degree. And of seeing that look on my friends' faces—like they were embarrassed for me because I couldn't hack a nine-to-five, like I was some sort of pariah."

Pariah? It was the exact right word. I was just about to fess up to my own deleterious love of books, when Shane pulled out the water bong I kept hidden between the couches. Without a word, he loaded it from his own sack. After offering it around (Kelly and I both declined), he charred the bowl and let the curling white smoke fill the green glass.

Then he exhaled a tremendous plume, coughed, and said, "I'll never leave OB, man. There's nothing else out there. You ask me, the rest of country may as well not even exist."

While I couldn't say I'd never leave Ocean Beach, I admitted that I'd found an unexpected peace in the community, that all my life I'd felt there was a part of me that was shameful and had to remain hidden. Somehow, OB took the edge off that feeling. Or maybe the place was just strange enough to distract me from myself?

"I wanted to be a writer," I said, and consciously avoided Kelly's eyes, "but that hadn't seemed possible in the small town where I grew up, where everybody was either a farmer or a factory worker. Let alone in the law school I drank my way through."

"Wait, you went to freaking *law* school?" Kelly said, and I remembered my interview with Jim and Juan Antonio, how they'd had more or less the same reaction.

While I probably couldn't ever fully escape the guy I'd tried to be—or pretended to be, or assumed I had to be, or was afraid of *not* being—maybe I could at least live in such a way that my past forays into conventionality would surprise the people I met. I explained how I'd felt like an imposter in my own skin, like I was living somebody else's life, and how in the end it all got so disheartening and stressful that I just sort of went crazy and took off.

Kelly touched my knee. "I know exactly what you mean—"

"Man," Shane said, still holding the leaking bong, "you lucked out by landing here. OB is a whole other country. A sovereign fuckin' nation of beautiful weirdos way out here on the sunburned bottom lip of America."

With that, I poured us all another round of Hornitos.

Later that night, Kelly snug in my bed with her warm thigh draped over my own and those lovely curls resting on our shared pillow, I heard the TV click on out in the living room. Then the rumble of Shane's mellow laughter.

≈

One slow night at Casa de Agave, Bentley took it upon himself to help me pass the time by explaining the tenets of Taoism and Confucianism in extraordinary detail. He must've spoken for two solid hours, highlighting philosophical and theological distinctions as I quartered limes, providing historical context while I mixed martinis, and explaining how these belief systems have influenced Eastern and Western thought as I rang in taco platters and restocked beer. Even now, after a decade of higher education, it remains the single most impressive monologue I've ever heard. After paying for his wine, Bentley rose from his stool, took a bow, and said, "Thanks for listening, friend."

Not to be outdone, Arturo began to bring me a succession of his favorite books, so that we might better wax philosophical about the meaninglessness of life. Nabokov and T. S. Eliot. Dostoevsky and García Márquez. Poppy Z. Brite and Cormac McCarthy. If it was dark or melancholy, Arturo adored it. As these book discussions unfolded and deepened, I came to understand that his disgust with the ignobility of human nature found some relief in literature, although he continued to insist the bombs really were about to fall.

On busy nights, these men sat across the small horseshoe bar from each other, and I'd feel their eyes on me, watching me pour, watching me sweat, but more so I felt the weight of our ongoing conversations. As the months passed, they told me about their lives, the details slipping out bit by bit, hour by hour, drink by drink.

As a penniless student, Bentley had lived in a camper trailer up the coast in La Jolla, eating rice and beans and studying molecular physics by flashlight. "It was the happiest period of my life, before or since," he said. "I learned everything I'll ever need to know about myself in that little camper."

Around the same age, Arturo's best friend stabbed him. They were at a beer party, cars parked in an arroyo, country music wailing in the sultry Texas night. No matter how intoxicated he became, no matter how morose, Arturo never would say exactly what led to the violence. One evening, brooding over his fifth or sixth cocktail, he said out of nowhere, "He stabbed me, dude. But he was my *friend*. He really was." Then he pulled out a baggie of painkillers and washed down a handful. When later he went to the restroom, I hid the baggie behind the cash register, a gesture for which he thanked me the following night.

Bentley once shot a stellar round at Torrey Pines. He strutted in afterward and I bought him a congratulatory glass of merlot. Beaming, he said that even when free our wine still tasted like piss—but that he'd tip anyway, considering I was now an honorary member of the family.

Arturo eventually convinced me to let him read my novel, that four-hundred page mess I'd written back in law school. He finished it in two days and had the heart to lie.

Bentley bought a copy of Gaiman's *American Gods* and slid it across the bar, like a tip.

Arturo's father chose not to visit him during the days and nights he lay in that Texas hospital with a near-fatal knife-wound in his back. He related this to me factually, dryly, maybe six months after we'd met, and with far less emotion in his voice than when he spoke of fiction.

～

Wonderland thrived for just two years, largely due to an unforeseen competitor— the California-Panama Exposition, which was located nearer the growing downtown—and the park soon fell into disuse and disrepair. The Tungsten lights darkened, and the dancing pavilion went silent and still. The Blue Streak Racer was disassembled and shipped up to Santa Monica, and the girders eventually crumbled into the Pacific. Finally, the exotic animals were leased to the Exposition, with the entire menagerie being later sold to the newly opened San Diego Zoo.

As it turned out, I lived in Wonderland for just two years as well. But the effect of place, particularly on our younger selves, is inestimable. Perhaps I'd understood this intuitively back when I first lit out for the West Coast, sensing in that sunset landscape a chance to discover, or maybe just accept, the person I apparently was.

Identity and geography are strange bedfellows, though. I'd felt like a hodad everywhere I'd ever been: as a boy, I lived in farming community but did not farm; in college, I lived in a fraternity house full of business majors but felt no real fraternity and abhorred the thought of studying business; while in law school I was the distracted and disaffected student who spent his nights and weekends clandestinely writing fiction. In the end, however, I rallied my courage and said to hell with all of that, only to wash up in OB. While I never did learn to surf, I nonetheless felt at home with the other misfits out there on the continent's lonely rim, at that place where there's nowhere left to run, and the exiles and castaways can just be.

Of course, there's a certain vanity in claiming outsider status. As if you were too pure or too sensitive for the social reality everyone else has to put up with. I won't dismiss my feelings quite so glibly, though. Because naïve as they were, those feelings drove me away from home and across a continent, for better or worse. It'd seemed to my younger self that what our culture had to offer was lacking in some crucial way. I couldn't have said how exactly—maybe I still can't, not ultimately—but having spent that time in Wonderland, I know I'm not alone.

So, here's to all the hodads out there. The outcasts and pariahs, the homeless who pick flowers and the dreamers and stoners and tenderhearted attorneys. The bibliophilic waitresses paying off student loans and the philosophy-loving, wine-quaffing physicists. Whenever I think of such people, I'm reminded of the day I moved into that ramshackle beach apartment. Before I'd even unpacked my laptop and books, I walked across the street and had an inaugural pint at The Tilted Stick.

"OB," read the sign, "WHERE THE DEBRIS MEETS THE SEA."

But such people are not debris. Not at all. And if they should flee certain places and gather in others, know that they're really just trying to survive—to put the necessary distance, both earthly and psychic, between themselves and whomever else this life demands they be.

5

LAST CALL AT PACIFIC SHORES

An Ocean Beach relic and institution, Pacific Shores—the same dive where I met Kelly and Shane—served no food, had no windows, and explicitly disallowed dancing. The drinks were gorilla strong and the restrooms a polluted miasma of things unspeakable. A lone door faced the tourist bustle along Newport Avenue, the breeze trickling in briny and sour. The walls featured neon aquatica (smiling octopus; busty mermaids; green-bearded merman) and a pair of giant fiberglass clam shells loomed over the bar, as if closing with imperceptible slowness upon the locals who wiled away their hours drinking in the salty gloom of a perpetual two a.m.

On the night in question, all I'd wanted was one more lousy beer at last call, but instead I got a double shot of the absurd. The place was packed and sweaty, three-deep along the rail. Some geek had quartered up a bunch of Elvis Costello, but the bartender (let's call him Joe) was too busy banging out drinks to skip the tracks. The lone cocktail waitress had given up battling the crowd and now loitered by the door, texting.

I hadn't realized the blonde woman seated in front of me (Sapphire? No, Daisy) was an exotic dancer, if an exotic dancer she actually was, until I heard Joe shouting for his bouncer to, "Get this stripper the hell outta here."

Enter said bouncer (Zeke) from stage left. Lean and wolfish, with oily black hair combed in a ducktail. Cratered cheeks, a broken nose, tattoo sleeves, chain wallet. You know the type.

"She's eighty-sixed," Joe said, pointing at Daisy, "for-fucking-ever."

Daisy glanced over her bare shoulder and her expression suggested in no uncertain terms that Zeke had best keep his paws to himself.

I did my best to make room, but the thirsty crowd kept pressing me forward.

"Come on, doll," Zeke said. "Let's pour you into a cab."

She shook her empty rocks glass in Joe's face and spoke a lone intelligible word—*vodka*—followed by a string of blackest obscenities.

"Time's up," Zeke said.

Daisy stood then. Teetering on her stilettos, she was almost as tall as me.

A peaceful resolution seemingly at hand, I resumed my futile efforts to catch Joe's eye and procure that all-important final beer. But Zeke didn't make it three steps before Daisy spun and chucked that forgotten rocks glass at Joe's face. A real heater, too. Thankfully, Joe had the reflexes to duck and spare his teeth. Still, the beveled glass ricocheted off the crown of his skull and shattered a backbar mirror.

Zeke was all over Daisy then, wrestling her toward the door in a hold that forced her arms up like a traffic cop. It was a pretty good move, but Daisy was wiry (pole-dancing?) and she eventually spun loose and seized him by the collar of his skintight Misfits T-shirt.

Then she lunged at his throat.

Fanged and aghast, Zeke loosed a piggy squeal I heard clearly over the blaring juke and can, in fact, still hear now. Finally, he managed to twist a fistful of Daisy's silken hair so tightly that her jaw fell open and her head canted aside, like a pussycat caught by the scruff.

The cocktail waitress ceased texting long enough to hold the door, and Zeke put the sole of his boot to Daisy's bottom and delivered her out into the night.

When I turned back to the bar, Joe was staring at me, the chaos having miraculously seen me to the head of the queue. A trickle of blood leaked down the side of Joe's face.

"You're bleeding," I said.

He dabbed at his cheek. "Shit. Hang on."

Then he wetted a small blue towel with vodka and pressed it to his lacerated scalp, no doubt wishing he'd just poured Daisy one more for the road and avoided all this insane carnage. Strangely, though, the scene had brought to mind a line from *The Bell Jar,* a book I'd read back in college in hopes of understanding my own dark feelings, about how the tasteless cold fire of vodka hits the stomach, "like a sword swallowers' sword," and leaves Plath's heroine feeling powerfully numb. But though that vodka may have numbed (or at least sterilized) his wound, Joe seemed in no mood for literary allusions; instead, he dug a frosty liter of Jägermeister from the cooler, zipped off the cap, poured two huge and treacly shots, and fired one down the oak to Zeke. Bleeding from his chewed neck, Zeke raised the glass in a weary salute.

Even then, more than a dozen years ago, part of me sensed the mindless and casual violence of that night would not easily be forgotten. It's the sort of weird and vaguely off-color bar story you feel strangely compelled to tell other people, despite knowing they may not really be all that interested, and even though (or perhaps because) it's so bombastic and seemingly without any clear takeaway, like a cosmic taunt; and when you do finally tell it, you inevitably do so while laughing and shaking your head, and this belies a grim seriousness—that sense you can't quite shake of some lesson or warning, a feeling that the veil parted oddly and for just a moment and you may have witnessed something meant for your eyes alone.

Beyond all that, though, or maybe beneath it, lay the drinking. So much booze, unquestioned and ever-present. Ocean Beach may have abutted the Pacific, but the community itself was afloat in a sea of alcohol. In OB, every weekend was a Lost Weekend, and as in Charles Jackson's slender novel of addiction, the drinks got tossed back faster than they could be counted, almost like breaths. And as for Pac Shores, the place was busy from the moment it opened in the morning until the last thirsty sot was whisked out the door.

But why? Why for so many of us, for me and seemingly everyone around me, did the constant drinking feel so necessary? Was it all just a bibulously irresponsible stage of life many people swim through, or were we all really self-medicating—trying to doubly inure ourselves by flooding our own bell jars with booze? Were we, like Jackson's alcoholic antihero Don Birnam, careening along on a self-destructive search for some indefinable and perhaps even nonexistent self-knowledge, a quest that ultimately reaches "the point where always there was only one thing: drink, and more drink"? Or was it, as Jean Rhys wrote, that having a drink made it feel as if the world weren't quite so proscribed, our days a little less despairingly predictable? What were we barflies ultimately searching for—or angling to duck or forget—by so continuously putting this thief into our mouths to steal our brains?

Stonefaced, Joe knocked back the Jäger. His eyes bore right through me, and his question, when it finally came, was a good one. "Last call, bro," he said. "What do you want?"

6

TERROIR

Oftentimes, though, the real question isn't what we want, but *who*—and late one night while counting down the till at Casa de Agave, I received an unexpected text: *Hey stranger...*

Rowan and I had dated throughout my final anxiety-riddled year of law school. Our breakup was hard but practical: her remaining year of legal studies, the relatively short time we'd been together, my desperate need to escape the monotony of Illinois and explore the West and try to become a writer. But we'd been good together while we lasted. Rowan was into hard rock, double gin and tonics, Stephen King novels, animal rights activism, and the wearing of *very* tight blue jeans—interests that had mirrored my own more or less seamlessly. In truth, looking back on law school, on those three interminably dull, dry, slogging, soulless years, Rowan was the only thing I missed. So, I was excited to hear from her, although as far as I knew she was still back in the Midwest practicing law. That, and she was engaged, or so said the grapevine.

Hey stranger...

A more prudent man surely would have ignored this midnight epistle. Would've assumed his former lover had in all likelihood simply poured herself one too many double gin and tonics. Would've recognized, sensibly, that nostalgia is a pleasure of memory alone.

I fired a text right back.

Soon, texting gave way to emails rehashing (revising, glossing over) our history, to discussions of dreams and goals and the frustrations and compromises of post-graduate life, to flirtations and what-ifs, to teasing and innuendo and hush-hush late-night phone calls.

Three weeks later, I picked Rowan up at San Diego Airport and drove us back to Ocean Beach. Sunset was near, and the view as we descended the Point Loma hills was idyllic: the sea-scoured shacks and glittering coastline, the silver-blue blanket of the Pacific, and the sky layered with streaks of gold and lavender and grenadine, like some exotic cocktail I might have whipped up on a lark.

"This place," Rowan said, admiring the palms and swells, the birds of paradise and trippy head shops, the dreadlocked and bikinied locals spilling from the streetside bars, "is so *not* the Midwest. It's like something from a Dr. Seuss book."

"Dr. Seuss on acid, maybe."

"It's amazing. I think I might love it." I glanced at her and smiled. "I really needed this," she said, still staring out the window.

A few days later, however, reality set in: this person had broken off an engagement, quit her job, and moved across the country—for me. Rowan was as I remembered, though: lovely, witty, and easygoing. Wanting to fit in around Ocean Beach, she went out straightaway and bought the skimpiest blue bikini available. She wore it day and night, like a vibrant counterpoint to my wrinkled board shorts and faded gray T-shirts. We reminisced about law school, the good times had between cramming for exams, the bad times endured living in that snowed-in and low-rent college town full of slum lords and chain restaurants and lackluster expectations, and soon it was as if we'd never broken up at all. As if we hadn't decided our connection wasn't enough, hadn't had relationships with other people, and hadn't pierced the brief bubble of sex and comfort and trust that'd been *us* back in Illinois.

In fact, we spent so much time fooling around in the surf and rubbing suntan lotion on each other's shoulders and licking tequila salt off each other's necks, that I ultimately decided to quit Casa de Agave and pursue beach-bummery full time. But rekindling romance wasn't my only motivation. Since moving to San Diego, I'd collected a number of classic novels I couldn't seem to get around to actually reading—in particular, Dickens and Melville. I'd dabbled in both back in college, but I hadn't really ingested them, hadn't read them once for story and once for theme and once again for their peculiar rhythm and voice, hadn't annotated them and dog-eared them and made them part of my permanent body of knowledge. And now, gainfully unemployed, it seemed if I could just manage to stay at least somewhat sober, I might finally plow headlong into my long-overdue education.

But somewhat sober I could not stay. No, Rowan and I lived a West Coast dream of endless sunshine, bottomless booze, and total joblessness. Our routine involved waking to tequila sunrises and icy bottles of Dos Equis at the bar down the block, eating mahi-mahi tacos at the restaurant across from the pier, wending our way down the sand and then swimming in the Pacific until we felt reborn, all before heading back to my bungalow to make lazy love and nap until dusk, whereupon we'd shower up and roam the local watering holes until last call.

Everything considered, life was good out there on the edge of the continent—although Rowan's ex certainly called a lot. He even tried to Facebook me. But I've never been much for social networking, so I politely declined his friend request.

By spring, however, our funds were running dry, and while San Diego had plenty of jobs, amid my Googling and Craigslisting I stumbled upon the Jenny Lake Lodge in Wyoming's Grand Teton National Park. A dude ranch back in the twenties, Jenny Lake was now a high-end destination complete with four-star dining. According to their ad, they needed a seasonal bartender, room and board and breathtaking vistas included. More specifically, they wanted someone with wine knowledge.

"Wait, do you even know anything about wine?" Rowan asked me.

The answer was a resounding not so much. Whiskies I knew well (probably *too* well), whereas I'd gotten acquainted with tequila in my time at Casa de Agave, and craft beer had long been of interest—but wine? Most of the wine I'd ever drunk had come out of a box.

I said something about faking it until one makes it.

"Since when do you even like wine, though?"

To which I responded that I'd always admired the grape just as much as the grain. Then she asked what was wrong with staying in Ocean Beach—it was vibrant and sunny and we both loved it, didn't we? And if I wanted to pour fancy wine, wasn't there a popular spot called 3rd Corner right around the block?

"It's great here," I said, "but I just can't concentrate." Then I launched into a litany of complaints as to why my writing wasn't going well: it was hard to even read a book, let alone write one, with Harley-Davidsons roaring past and drunken revelers stumbling by at all hours and our upstairs neighbors dealing coke every night until four a.m. Yes, OB was fun, a lot of fun, but I was afraid if I didn't escape the fun I'd end up like that booze-haunted dipsomaniac Don Birnam, a man desperate enough to hock my typewriter (well, my laptop) for drinking money, only to drunkenly tumble down the stairs and wake up in the alcoholic ward suffering wildly solipsistic delusions straight out of a story by Edgar Allan Poe...

Yet OB was a place that Rowan was totally enamored with, a place that had woken her from the malaise she'd fallen into back in the Midwest, and the conflict showed on her face. But she trusted me and believed in me, and we'd been so good together—both back in Illinois and here in California—that I couldn't help but feel my dreams necessarily dovetailed with her own, and that we'd be okay no matter where we went. So long as we stayed together this time, what could go wrong?

Long story short, I phoned the lodge at Jenny Lake, was hired by a prickly sounding English woman, negotiated Rowan a hostessing job, and found a friend in L. A. willing to cat-sit Bart for the summer. In the days to come, fantasies of writing amid silent mountain woods budded in my imagination. No more crowds, no snarling traffic, no flight-path roar—just read, write, hike, and pour fine wine for five pristine months. I thought of old Henry Thoreau going to the woods to simplify and live deliberately, to suck life's marrow, conscientiously object to whatever needed objecting to, and keep that extraordinary journal. While I wasn't quite ready for the life of an abstemious hermit, I did imagine soaking up inspiration from the mountain wilderness, the better to finally go more confidently in the direction of a literary life. That these were the very same ambitions that had driven me away from a career in law in the first place—and away from Illinois and Rowan—somehow didn't register as a potential impediment.

A few nights later, packing boxes, Rowan asked if I'd miss California.

Even before deciding to leave, I'd known exactly how she felt about Ocean Beach—that it was love at first sight, the place she'd needed to quell her own discontent with the person she'd found herself becoming back home. But for me, home had become a foreign concept, terra incognita on my interior map—or maybe, as James Baldwin puts it, you don't really have a home until you've left it, but once you've left you can never go back—so I ducked the question by reminding her that in Wyoming we'd have our very own private cabin, peace and quiet, mountain views and wildlife and so on and so on, until finally she just smiled and kissed me.

≈

According to the artist Thomas Moran, who trekked the Rockies to take sketchings for *The Three Tetons,* his 1895 painting that now hangs in the Oval Office, "The Tetons have loomed up grandly against the sky . . . perhaps the finest pictorial range in the United States."

But heading north from Jackson, our initial views of this fine pictorial range—one glacier-covered peak of which is named after Moran—were blocked by a big brown butte. To the east, herds of pronghorn antelope flowed like schooling fish across the sagebrush-covered valley. Not until we'd climbed higher did the Tetons appear. One moment we were listening to the radio and navigating the curves, when suddenly a forty mile wall of ice-capped teeth cut the horizon. Due to a lack of foothills and the valley floor's curious tilt, the peaks seemed perilously cantilevered over the roadway.

"Holy smokes," Rowan said, and took my hand.

"Told you it'd be special," I said.

The sky shimmered like burnished metal as sunset drenched the range in a fender-bending Technicolor spectacle to rival even the best of sunsets back in Ocean Beach. Highway 89 was thick with traffic, as well, and cheeky signs spaced every hundred yards reminded motorists to obey the speed limit: "Wildlife ahead! / That Means Go Slow! / That Bull Moose . . . / Is Some Cow's Beau!" And slow it was, as every time a moose (or any other exotically large ungulate) wandered within camera distance of the highway, traffic totally stalled.

"Don't take this the wrong way," Rowan said, after we'd hit yet another wildlife jam, "but I never saw myself working in a restaurant after law school."

A bit taken aback, I assured her that our jobs were just for the summer. We'd have no bills—think of all the cash we'd save. Then I pointed at the cathedral-like mountain range and prismatic sunset. "Besides, this is once in a lifetime, right?"

"I mean, there's nothing wrong with that sort of work, but—"

"Look!" I pointed. "A wolf!"

She squinted. "I'm pretty sure that's just a coyote." Moments later, we passed the scrawny gray dog loping parallel to the road. "There were coyotes in my yard back in Illinois," she said.

But there weren't mountains in Illinois, and the closer we came to them, the closer we came to our summer home. We reached the lodge just before dark. The ground was still snow-tracked in May, the high-altitude air biting, the grove of lodgepole pines surrounding the cabins towering and gloomy. Our accommodations proved as rustic as promised. Serenaded by the mournful howling of what were most definitely wolves, Rowan and I spent that first night bundled in our warmest clothes and sipping nostalgically from a bottle of tequila. But as the night wore on, it became clear that our "private" cabin was actually one cabin split in two, with only a flimsy plywood divider separating us from our neighbor, a cook. If ears did not deceive, this cook enjoyed adult cartoons, suffered a sinus infection, and ate a high-fiber diet. Rowan, bless her, pretended not to notice any of this.

I'd known we were facing an adjustment, but a good and necessary one. Dawn would be rejuvenating, with clean sunrays hitting the snow-capped peaks just outside our door. We'd get up early for coffee and a hike. Healthy living in the crisp, clean air. No more breakfast beers and no more all-night benders. But sometime in the wee hours of that first night, I awoke to screams.

As I fumbled for the bedside flashlight, Rowan thrashed awake in a cocoon of blankets and said, "What the *hell?*" Which was my thought exactly. The screaming was loud and close, seemingly just outside. I pulled on my Nikes and pushed through the door into the icy darkness, half-expecting to find a wolf or even a grizzly mauling one of our new coworkers. Instead, on the porch of a neighboring cabin, my flashlight beam revealed a young woman dressed in grandfatherly blue pajamas. She leaped up and down in a panic, squealing and raking her fingers through her hair. I called out, but the woman merely stared saucer-eyed into the wobbly flashlight beam and shrieked at me in a South African accent. Then she vaulted the porch steps and fled up the path toward the main lodge. Moments later, I heard a door slam shut.

Back in the cabin, I told Rowan what I'd seen. "Well, I hope she's all right," she said, but she just as easily might have said, "Well, that was a bad omen. . ."

The next morning, talk around the breakfast table was that this woman, a concierge, had packed and left at sunup. "First casualty of the season," one of the veteran employees put it. An investigation of the vacated cabin revealed the recent thaw had enlivened a clutch of maggots feeding upon something gone mushy in the attic space. Carrion-fat larvae had rained down upon the young concierge in her sleep, wriggling and milky, landing in her hair, in the cups of her ears and her open mouth, like a nightmare straight out of Revelation.

~

But the employee cabins were a pleasure compared to the bar, which was a dungeon worthy of Alexandre Dumas. Missing only a lice-infested straw mat and rusty manacles, it smelled of dust and the ammoniac sweat of previous inmate-bartenders. A series of notches marred the sink table—probably just nicks from cutting fruit, but also not unlike the marks a prisoner might make while counting down the days. The space was so confined that, arms outstretched, I could easily grab liquor bottles from either wall. But wine, not liquor, was the mainstay at Jenny Lake, and for a restaurant at seven thousand feet in a national park, the lodge offered an impressive list. Jenny wasn't the destination for working-class families from Ohio determined to see a moose, but for jet-setters and old money.

The swankier cabins approached a thousand dollars nightly, and come dinner, the guests washed down fifty-dollar plates of roast elk with two-hundred-dollar bottles of Bordeaux. A massive wine fridge kept the vintages cool, but also pumped out torrents of electrical heat. Cobwebs lay thick over everything. Enough to make Miss Havisham croak with glee.

Prior to arrival, I'd been informed by Audrey, the general manger, that I'd be working a service bar—meaning no guest seating, a bar dedicated exclusively to filling the dining room orders—but I'd convinced myself this would be relaxing. Burned out by the raucous San Diego bar scene, I'd thought a service bar sounded nice. But this wasn't nice. The stale closet had one miniature window where I placed the finished drinks—a window through which a warden might cuff a convict's wrists—and I enjoyed no view of anything other than fast-closing walls and dusty bottles. It wasn't quite solitary confinement, though, as my cell was shared by a family of little gray mice.

Audrey and her assistant, a local named Howard, provided me with traps, both of the glue and guillotine varieties, and every time I heard that sharp report, my heart sank. The spring-traps didn't always kill, you see. No, it was the lucky mouse that found its organs shooting out in bloody jets from mouth and anus, as most were merely maimed—left with their head half-crushed or a foreleg smashed to ribbons—and spent their final moments in terrified and bloody agony, dragging around a patch of peanut-butter-smeared balsa wood.

"Got one!" Howard would exclaim, anytime he was within earshot of a sprung trap.

As a salaried employee, Howard thought himself above cleaning up the crippled little victims, so it was left to Jenny Lake's newest bartender (later I would discover that no bartender had ever returned for a second season) to take a slug of whiskey and employ his shoe, to suffer the feel of mincing bones beneath the sole. However commonplace this chore, the splattering of those cute but decidedly unhygienic little bundles never got any easier. But seeing the little fellows stuck and quivering on those sadistic glue pads, button eyes shining, exhausted hearts suffering under delicate ribs, was somehow even worse. After a long week of this, I gathered all the remaining traps and tossed them out.

When Howard noticed, he questioned me. And when I gave my reply, which was that Mouseschwitz would have to find another overseer, Howard and I reached a silent but mutual agreement to never again have anything remotely approaching a friendly conversation. Also, Howard had a crush on Rowan, which he did little to conceal. "You're a *lawyer?*" he'd say, following her around and staring at her ass. "Wow, you're almost too pretty to be a lawyer. Think you might like to settle down and practice here in Wyoming?" Anytime I dared step foot outside the dungeon, especially if Rowan was around, Howard would instantly materialize at my side and request that I return to the service bar immediately.

Finally, I decided the only way to cope was with books. But the first time Audrey caught me reading—*A Tale of Two Cities,* no less—she frowned in her distinctly English way, as if she'd caught a whiff of offal, and asked if I actually believed that reading *Dickens* on the clock was appropriate. When I responded that I saw little choice *but* to read Dickens on the clock, she suggested that I might better consider my janitorial duties. "Look at that floor," she said. "It's filthy."

A glance at the tiles revealed that she was right. But I merely shrugged, as if the floor's dirtiness was a subjective phenomenon, the need to sweep and mop a matter for debate. A week before, I'd witnessed Audrey march outside and shoo away a juvenile grizzly that was snacking on the lodge's shrubbery. Waving her arms and stomping toward the blockish and fuzzy oaf, she'd shouted, "Bear! Bear! You will cease molesting those huckleberry bushes this instant!" So, yes, Audrey was formidable in the way of small, dogged persons, but if she took away my reading privileges, I knew I'd never last the season. I held her narrow blue eyes, a finger keeping my place in the novel, and Audrey stared back like a gunslinger for four or five unblinking seconds—an absurdly long time under the circumstances—until she finally gave a resigned "Harrumph!" and walked away.

For all its faults, though, the dungeon proved a fine place to read. I spent the early hours of my shifts studying up on wine from the tomes in the prison library, but late nights were dedicated to the classics. A typical evening saw me dispense glasses of pinot and cabernet through the jailer's window, all while Dickens foreshadowed the bloodshed of the French Revolution via a cask of red wine broken and pooling on those Parisian cobblestones.

"Audrey may be okay with you reading," Howard said one night, "but I really don't think—"

"It was the best of jobs, and it was the worst of jobs."

"If you've got this much free time you should really go help bus tables."

"It was the easiest of jobs"—I flipped the page without even a glance Howard's way—"and the dullest of jobs."

But my patience waned as I struggled through *David Copperfield.* Despite my sympathizing with the class struggle—moonlighting as a bartender will make one do that—the brick-thick tome chronicling young David's quest to see whether he will indeed become the hero of his own pages (great line, obvious answer) mercifully gave way to *Moby-Dick*.

"Now that's certainly an odd book," Audrey said one night, while passing by my cell. "Melville was quite the eccentric, wasn't he? Imagine what his publisher must've thought when they realized half the novel is just a thinly veiled fetishization of fishing gear."

Amused, I mentioned a passage I'd just read, which concerned a lanced whale. Melville, clearly no more the oenophile than I, compares the spurting blood not to wine, as might seem obvious, but to good red American whiskey. But Audrey merely gave me an assertive stink-eye before bustling off, as she couldn't have the rest of the staff thinking they could indulge their hobbies mid-shift. Restaurants are much like whaling ships in this way: there's very little tolerance for insubordination. Audrey was clearly Ahab, and Howard was Starbuck, and if I insisted on being Ishmael, so be it. But the rest of the staff would have to keep right on swabbing the deck and refilling bread baskets, lest we find ourselves sinking mid-summer.

Those unfortunate servers would burst upon the jailer's window, panicked and sweaty from their nightly haranguing courtesy of the well-to-do guests, only to find me engrossed in a novel. This caused some to lash out in frustration—which I ignored, much as I ignored the scurrying mice, much as I ignored Howard—while others felt compelled to share stories of how much more difficult their lives were than mine, how high-maintenance and stingy the guests were, how they were just a bunch of cranky old rich bastards.

Listening to these complaints it occurred to me that Jenny Lake's guests were like the Monseigneur, Dickens's vile and sybaritic French aristocrat who requires four servants merely to feed him his breakfast chocolate. Since I was unable to see it, I could only imagine the dining room, and in my mind's eye it was peopled not with investment bankers and heiresses dressed in freshly purchased North Face gear, but with lip-smacking ghouls with powdered cheeks and frizzled wigs, all done up in silk and brocade. Had these elites run over a baby moose in their Mercedes SUVs, they'd have quite possibly handled it much like the Monseigneur does upon crunching a peasant boy under the wheels of his speeding carriage—by tossing a few coins at the grieving (moose) parents before checking to make sure the tires weren't damaged.

So, yeah, I felt bad for the servers. But how could they fail to realize they were interrupting my reading?

~

As hostess, however, Rowan was constantly visible and therefore couldn't console herself with books. In fact, she despised her job and made her feelings clear by leaving me to sleep alone while she partied with the other employees. Hard to blame her, really. The whole trying excursion—the dinky cabin, the mice, our onanistic neighbor and his pornographic anime—all was my glorious brainchild. But regressing to how we'd lived in Ocean Beach, to the constant hangovers and lost time, didn't feel like the right move, either.

One night after the last seating, Rowan walked by the service cell and knocked on the pass-through. I glanced up. "You hold those books right in front of your face," she said, "like your own little wall."

I lowered the book just in time to see her walking away.

Still, after a couple months of steady reading, I felt detoxed. I rose clearheaded at dawn for powdered eggs and coffee, before hiking the nearby trails to Hidden Falls and Inspiration Point. Then it was back to the cabin to write until early afternoon. What I was working on back then (think Stephen King if he'd read too much Cormac McCarthy) wasn't ultimately much more than a prolonged literary throat-clearing, but at least it was better than the novel I'd scribbled in the guard shack back in Illinois. So, progress of a sort. And I was feeling better, more sober. The day's writing finished, I'd take a long run past fields of blooming lupine and monkshood under the watchful gazes of Mount Owen and Teewinot. Then it was off to the dungeon for another round with the classics.

This routine was ideal in a lot of ways—but ideal for me, not Rowan. With each passing week, she grew unhappier, and short of just packing up and heading back to San Diego, which was financially unfeasible, I didn't know how to fix things. But surely the beauty of the place, the majestic peaks and crystalline lakes and unsullied forests, would sustain us through season's end. My ad hoc wine education seemed to support this optimism, as well. In particular, a conversation had with Audrey, who was a full-fledged sommelier.

"French winemakers bet the house on terroir," she said, after we'd received our weekly shipment of bottles. "That's part of what makes French wines so interesting." I'd come across this curious term—*terroir*—in my reading but glossed over it. Audrey noticed my hesitation and explained how these winemakers placed faith not so much in technique, but in the land itself. "Wine can seem intimidating," she said, "but it's quite simple, really. Think of it as geology—as climate and time and soil—naked in the glass."

This conversation led me back to the wine books with renewed interest. As Audrey had said, Old World vintners trust that the same character of wine simply could not be produced elsewhere. Burgundy, for example, contains the perfect combination of climate, topography, and elevation for growing pinot noir—a grape selected for its subtlety and lightness in the belief that land and weather, the slightest variations in temperature and sun, will better shine through. We aren't all sommeliers, though, and most of us can't tell Côte d'Or from Beaujolais, and many of us can't tell either of those from a decent table wine—or even a bottle of plonk. Still, the idea of terroir echoed, like something I'd felt all my life but lacked the necessary word for. Medieval Cistercian monks gleaned the concept from the writings of ancient Egyptians and Classical-era Greeks, who'd noticed certain tracts of land tended to produce certain qualities of wine. Add to this more figurative notions, such as those of the geologist James E. Wilson, who writes, "Beyond the measurable ecosystem, there is an additional dimension— the spiritual aspect that recognizes the joys, the heartbreaks, the pride, the sweat, and the frustrations of its history."

Terroir isn't the only factor in play, though. There's also the simple daily care required to maintain something inherently fragile. Consider the evening Audrey came to the service cell with a freshly opened and very expensive bottle and asked me for a clean glass. After pouring a little, she swirled, sniffed, tasted, and said, "What a shame—oxidized."

A wine's flavors unlock with exposure to air, hence the haughty-seeming swirling, but the oxidization process begins immediately. Properly cared for, a good wine will keep for decades, but once the cork is pulled, its charms must be appreciated in the moment.

Audrey frowned and set the bottle aside. "Put this down the sink, will you?"

I hesitated, thinking of the cost.

"Go on," she said. "There's nothing to be done about it now."

≈

One of the lodge's most popular vintages was a pinot noir from Domaine Drouhin. The vineyard is owned by a French winemaker but rests in Oregon's Willamette Valley. Faint ruby in color and with an aroma of cedar, this wine— savored from a handy coffee mug—made an excellent complement to my nightly reading. The Willamette Valley is ideal for growing pinot. Cool but rarely cold.

Warm and sunny but seldom hot. Damp, but blessed with naturally draining soil. Conditions that encourage the delicate and subtle, the webbed and allusive. Qualities necessary for a certain type of wine and perhaps, I was coming to believe, for a certain type of life.

The more delicate the wine, however, the more careful need be the handling. Because oxidization isn't the only danger. Light can also harm wine, as ultraviolet rays interact with sulfur components to give off a cardboard flavor. No matter the vintage, no matter if the grapes were harvested from the best regions, and regardless of measures taken to optimize fermentation and maturation, just a few careless seconds and what could have been lovely and special is ruined.

Such was the state of my wine knowledge when, a few weeks later, I awoke to find Rowan sitting up in bed, clutching her wrist to her chest. I had no memory of her returning to the cabin the night before. She'd been out late again, partying away her anxieties.

"You're holding that arm like a lame paw," I said.

And then she admitted how, at some point in the evening, she'd performed a backward handstand. A series of backward handstands, actually. "On a stupid dare," she added. I asked the obvious questions, to which she replied, "I guess I just wanted to prove I could still do it."

From the sound of things, I wasn't the only one wondering if time was passing them by. But somehow Rowan and I couldn't manage to communicate these shared worries. If anyone could understand people like us, surely it was *us*, yet a wall of silence had sprung up, one even taller and thicker than the book-wall I'd built in the wine dungeon.

"Well, you apparently still can do backward handstands," I said. "But I'm not so sure about your arms."

She laughed but grimaced at the pain it cost her. "Thanks, smartass."

Already pulling on my jeans, I said we'd better go find a doctor.

She eased her way from the bed. "*Are* there doctors up here?"

Indeed there were, and an X-ray taken at an orthopedic clinic in Jackson confirmed she'd fractured her radius. It would likely heal without surgery, but the break was in a sensitive spot and needed monitoring—new X-rays every two weeks, minimum. Over beers at a cowboy bar, Rowan's arm in a flimsy sling that cost us a combined day's wages, we mulled over our options.

"We can't keep paying three-hundred bucks," she said, "to have a doctor look at me for ten seconds and tell me my arm's broken."

"I should've gone to medical school. It's a license to steal."

"But then you wouldn't have time to read and write your books," she said.

While this might have been a barb, and a sharp one, she hadn't meant it that way. I asked what we should do, and she mentioned going back to Ocean Beach. We'd given up our apartment there, though, and I'd given up my job, and the medical care situation would've been much the same: uninsured, unaffordable, out of reach. Our conversation went on like that through another round of beers, beating around the sagebrush, until we finally said the hell with it and started ordering whiskies.

Corked wine is probably the best-known wine fault. It results from the interaction of chlorine, typically found in cleaning agents, with certain fungi present in cork. Corked wines taste dull and soggy, the fruit's brightness lost. Now that the problem is better understood, the industry avoids chlorine-based cleansers, and the incidence has fallen. It remains the most familiar term, though, and so other faults, such as those caused by air or light or whatever else, get blamed on the innocent little cork. All this just goes to show how delicate wine truly is. Unlike whiskey or tequila, for example, where high proofage ensures the mature spirit never changes, wine is alive in the bottle. It's dynamic, constantly evolving. Even the exact same vintage can't be experienced twice in quite the same way, but subtly necessitates thoughtful and gentle handling, because Audrey was right: once something has spoiled, there really is nothing to be done.

So, a few weeks later, when Rowan's brothers called to say they just happened to be touring Yellowstone, we decided it would be best if they swung by the cabin and picked her up. After loading her suitcases, she and I stood on the porch in the shadow of the mountains.

"I'll see you once the season's over," she said.

"You bet."

"My father's thinking of retiring soon." Her father was an attorney, as well. Small-town Illinois. Divorces, land disputes, wills. Rowan and her mother had been discussing the family business over the phone recently, the changes coming and what they might mean. "He's going to need someone to take over the firm," she said.

I thought then of the town where I was born, an unremarkable place just a couple of hours from Rowan's equally unremarkable hometown, and I remembered the endless Melvillian sea of cornfields, the map of isolated rural communities like islands dotting a blanket of windblown green, the labyrinthine piping of four-story grain silos like the masts and rigging of clipper ships, and, above all, that sense of conservative claustrophobia it had taken me many years and many miles to finally leave behind. The Midwest is a perfectly decent place, of course, but its terroir simply won't produce a decent wine. Similarly, I wondered about the bohemian bacchanal of Ocean Beach, the farthest possible place from where I'd—where we'd—grown up, both geographically and spiritually. And finally, the mountains, the cold, thin air, the direct quality of light, the nights tipped with frost. These landscapes we passed through had also passed through us, and maybe we hadn't navigated the terrain as similarly as I'd believed.

Then we said we loved each other and kissed goodbye. As I watched Rowan disappear into the back of that car, I was still hopeful things might work out, and we did try for a time, but I sensed even then that what we'd had, for whatever reasons, had turned.

7

ROGUES, REVOLUTION, AND RENAISSANCE

In the fall of 2008, back in the Northwest after that summer in the Tetons, I landed at a Portland taphouse called the Green Dragon.

The curious name was an ode to Boston's historic Green Dragon Tavern. It was from this colonial period watering hole that the Sons of Liberty—a group of revolutionaries founded by Samuel Adams[3]—sipped ale from the massive Liberty Bowl (engraved by a local silversmith named Paul Revere) and hatched plans to dress up like Mohawks and steep British tea in saltwater. In 1775, this same Green Dragon was where Revere began his famous midnight ride to Lexington. And I was to discover that Portland's Green Dragon was hatched with revolution in mind, as well—but against the moneyed forces coalescing in the craft beer movement, those "big" microbrewers that many perceived as a threat to the independent spirit of artisanal beer culture.

The Dragon stood on a graffiti-tagged corner in the Southeast industrial district. Out back was a beer garden strung with lights and fenced off by chain-link topped with concertina wire. A seedy-looking olive drab Quonset hut, long rumored either a heroin den or a pornographic film set (if not both), completed the scene. Inside it was minimalist, with a concrete bar and exposed rafters and a small stage for live music. Curios were sprinkled about: a taxidermied armadillo, a blowfish lamp, and a stuffed donkey with a tampon protruding sadly from its felt anus.

Otherwise, the Dragon was just a half-renovated warehouse—although a warehouse with twenty taps lining the wall (as well as a "secret" twenty-first tap for the rarest of beers), and not one hooked to a keg produced in St. Louis, Milwaukee, or Golden, Colorado.

The tap list was on a chalkboard high above the bar. Whenever a keg popped, a bartender would grab the pulley ropes and lower the board wobbling and squeaking down to eye-level, before chalking in the next keg and then hauling it back up hand over fist. Performing this chore or seeing it performed, I was

---

3 Two centuries later, Adams would become the namesake of a successful Boston-based craft brewery.

always reminded of those sailors on the *Pequod* hauling buckets of whale oil up to the deck from the freshly harpooned carcass lashed amidships.

In fact, the Dragon's crew proved colorfully Melvillian. There was the impeccably coiffed lead bartender with debonair manners and a wardrobe full of casually moth-eaten sweaters; pair him with Gamby, a six-foot-five and three-hundred-pound sidekick who wore combat boots and sported a ZZ Top beard, and you had quite the duo. There was also a waitress who practiced the reiki arts, a hollow-eyed guy who sulked around reading grizzled paperbacks by Hunter Thompson, and Sabrina Pepper, a feisty redhead who dressed like a boy in old Levis and Reeboks, the better to charm the hopheads and beer geeks (honorifics, not insults) whose bar talk was more likely to concern dry-hopping, or the effervescent mouth feel attendant secondary fermentation than, say, the Blazers chances to make the playoffs.

For entertainment, the Dragon employed the services of Howlin' Bob Shoemaker. An old-school blues hound, Howlin' Bob favored steel guitar, did a rousing *Jolie Blon*, and liked to wet his impressively loud whistle with a few drinks—but he wasn't the only musician around.

Max (barback), Sid (dishwasher), and Anders (cook) all slacked through school together and now shared a house where their Nordic black metal band— Sexecutioner—practiced in the basement. Sid was suitably dark and brooding, while Anders and Max each sported witchy black hair, pointy goatees, and gave Queequeg a run for his money in the tattoo department, although their ink consisted mainly of pentagrams and 666s and various demons and occult creatures.

I came to work at this eccentric spot courtesy of a friend named Abbott who'd managed the Steelhead Bar & Grill (Gary, the manager who'd initially hired me, was soon thereafter fired—hopefully for reasons unrelated to hiring inexperienced, résumé-faking bartenders). But Abbott and I had kept in touch in the years since, and one day shortly after leaving Jenny Lake, while I sat drinking in a Jackson saloon with candelabras fashioned from elk antlers and buffalo heads mounted on the walls, my phone rang.

"I'm cooking up a tasty stew here, Philbert," Abbott said. "It's really perfect this time."

Sure enough, the Green Dragon did seem perfect. The staff was bursting with countercultural inclinations, the regulars were true-blue beer people, and there were no rules whatsoever. The political climate was right for it, too, as Barack Obama's historic campaign had energized the entire city. On the Dragon's triumphant election night bash, flyers were hung with Obama's face Photoshopped together with the noble countenance of Abraham Lincoln.

Hope and change were in the air. You could almost taste it.

⌇

Portland's so-called craft beer revolution launched in the mid-eighties, led by ambitious homebrewers such as Kurt and Rob Widmer (of hefeweizen fame), and Mike and Brian McMenamin, who today own a chain of Grateful Dead-inspired brewpub and hotel venues throughout the Northwest. Before craft beer found its niche in the American palate, however, Anheuser-Busch, Miller, and Coors had so thoroughly dominated the market that few Americans even realized beer needn't be pale yellow and bodiless—or that its taste needn't necessarily evoke the excretions of those famous Clydesdales.

But corporate lager's dominance was a relatively new phenomenon. Prior to the passage of the Eighteenth Amendment and the inception of Prohibition in 1920, American beer styles varied by region, influenced by the brewing traditions of European immigrants. In late-nineteenth-century Portland, for example, Henry Weinhard's brewery was producing dark and hearty beers similar to those of his native Germany. But the hardships of World War I and Prohibition shut down nearly all the independent brewers. Only the largest and most cutthroat managed to survive, which led to an ethos of bigger and blander. English porters and bitters, a staple since colonial days, were forgotten, along with the more esoteric Belgian-style ales and sours.

From that point forward, American beer was made as cheaply as possible in a simple lager style, and brewers came to look less like craftsmen and more like steel barons. Hence, a half-century of mass industrialization, monopolization, and disinformation, the result of which was an ocean of subpar beer. Much like the oily gin foisted upon the proletariat in *1984*, to drink corporate lager was done not for taste, but for effect alone.

Thankfully, there was a secret resistance: home brewers. And when President Carter finally legalized homebrewing in the late seventies (it'd been banned since Prohibition), the states were free to amend their laws such that independent brewers could open pubs and sell their unique beer. But it wasn't just that this "microbrew" tasted better; it also had a different philosophy. The people who made it seemed more concerned with artfulness than getting rich, and the advertising was nothing like the propaganda disseminated by Big Beer—Spuds

Mackenzie and the Swedish Bikini Team and endless appeals linking colorless, odorless, flavorless, characterless beer with the very spirit of the nation.

So, it made sense that people came to refer to the rise of craft beer as a "revolution." But the term implies something new—a new nation, new identity, new ideas—and it also implies politics and social tumult, if not even violence. Was that really the proper way to describe the work of those craftsmen brewers who'd revived a host of forgotten beer styles? Was making and enjoying the same good beer that'd been parcel to western culture for hundreds—or, in the case of ale more broadly, for thousands of years—really an act of defiance, or something else?

$\approx$

Not long after I'd started at the Dragon, however, and before the young President-elect even took office, Abbott called and asked to meet for morning coffee. When I found him, he was outside a pub reading *The Oregonian* and sipping not coffee, but a pint. I soon found out why.

Rogue Ales, one of the most successful craft brewers in Oregon, had tendered an offer for the Dragon.

"They're just a bunch of frat boys who got lucky," he said. "You been down to their place in Newport?" When I told him I hadn't, he said it was corny and garish. "They make decent beer, but they're ruthless and greedy. They'd be just as happy selling sheets of tin. They'll ruin everything that's special about the Dragon—mark my words."

I ordered a pint of my own and then asked why the owner would considering selling in the first place, with the Dragon building such a loyal following.

"Money trouble," Abbott said. "What else?"

Then he explained the owner was a dot-com guy, and that most of his wealth was on paper. With the tech bubble having burst and the housing and banking crises tanking the economy, most of that funny money had vanished. "So, now his wife wants him to sell his little hobby," Abbott said, "and put them back on the road to early retirement."

I asked if anything could be done. There were a few minority owners, after all. What was their plan? And the craft beer community would surely offer whatever support it could. But Abbott didn't seem to hear me. "It was the perfect stew," he said. "It had everything."

$\approx$

While Abbott drank that breakfast beer out of frustration and anxiety, he was on solid historical footing. Back in medieval times, water quality was such that Europeans of all ages and social classes had little choice but to drink fermented (i.e., sterile) beverages at all hours of the day, at risk of contracting cholera or dysentery or some other waterborne bug. The beer of this time was largely brewed at home and thought of as food. Old folks drank beer, children drank beer, lords and ladies alike drank beer. The overall volume was a fraction of today's output, of course, but consumption per person far outstripped even the beeriest of modern demographics.

And the beer these people drank was different, too. Before the widespread use of hops as a bittering agent in the thirteenth and fourteenth centuries, along with purity laws such as the Bavarian *Reinheitsgebot* and Pasteur's later work on fermentation science, beer was far less uniform. Instead of hops, for instance, beer was spiced with a concoction known as gruit that's recipe varied dramatically, and wild yeast and bacteria would've imparted a certain unpredictable character. One question is the extent to which such variation and irregularity was artful in its own right, or at least left room for art, as opposed to the industrial standardization of twentieth-century beer prior to the craft beer revolution—a revolution at least partially defined by a revival of the very "mistakes" technology and industrialization nearly did away with entirely.

Along with such questions comes an analogy: because while the beer of the Middle Ages was safer to drink than water, the medieval church—often involved in the monastic brewing of that same beer—was far from safe. With an iron grip on social and political power, it conditioned an illiterate and downtrodden body of serfs to believe their lives were inherently sinful and fallen, worldly pleasures but a snare opening their souls to hellfire, and submission and mortification to a god they couldn't understand the only route to salvation; whereas Big Beer conditioned a downtrodden body of working people to forget the simple joy they'd once taken in real beer and to trust their fleeting pleasures to the well-fed acolytes of a modern trinity of mechanization, mass production, and homogenization.

～

A month later, I was down in Sexecutioner's practice cave, admiring the underworld ambiance—*Hellraiser* and *Evil Dead* posters, tombstones plundered from a nearby cemetery, a battle-axe ordered off QVC while shit-faced at three a.m.—when Sid the dishwasher came clomping downstairs with a handle of Everclear, a couple of Bud tallboys, and a critique of the Dragon's new ownership.

"If Rogue thinks I'm gonna start wearing a nametag and acting like Howdy Doody," he said, "they're in for a big surprise."

As it turned out, Abbott's fears were warranted; the Dragon's majority owner had extricated himself from the bar business by selling out to Rogue Ales. In the wake of the buyout, Abbott was canned, Gamby and many of the other original staff members quit, Howlin' Bob found another gig, and the beer geeks emitted a collective moan. The sense was that Big Brother had hijacked a treasured outpost. In fact, a group of beer activists actually published a "declaration of war" aimed at the Rogue Nation (a marketing ploy whereby Rogue provides incentives to visit its pubs), and there was much craft beer-fueled talk of lawsuits and boycotts and industrial sabotage, none of which ended up amounting to much.

After carefully aiming a BB pistol and shooting Sid—who still had his hands full—square in the forehead, Anders said, "Yeah, it totally sucks to work for Rogue."

But he did have to admit that the newly offered employee health insurance would allow him to afford the seven-hundred-fifty-dollar bifocals upgrade he desperately needed.

Max, after cursing Rogue as a bunch of capitalist fist-fuckers, said, "It'll be nice to pour beers and make tips, though. Instead of just washing pints and scrubbing toilets."

And Sid—after disarming Anders and brutally pistol-whipping him across the shoulder blades—confessed that he didn't really give a shit who signed his paychecks, so long as he got to keep reading his Cthulhu mythos in the dish pit. "But seriously," he added, "they can stick their nametags where the sun don't shine."

As for me, I missed Abbott and my old coworkers. I'd thought about leaving, too, for solidarity's sake, but refusing to work for Rogue was impractical, as my car still needed gasoline and my landlady still expected rent come the first of the month.

Then Anders prepared a round of Sexecutioner's traditional cocktail: the POE, or Potion of Evil. I watched him crack a tall boy and splash Budweiser into four grimy glasses. Then he squeezed an eyedropper of liquid THC into each one, before uncapping the Everclear brand 190-proof grain neutral spirits—more industrial solvent than palatable beverage—and topping the Mephistophelian concoction with boiler-making shots of highly flammable liquor.

"Bottoms up," he said.

But I pushed my potion to the center of the table.

"You narcing out on us, college boy?"

I explained that as a Green Dragon employee, as an ambassador of craft beer and all things local and artisanal, it seemed hypocritical to drink an Anheuser-Busch product.

"Yeah, but now we all work for Rogue, and they're just as bad."

"Are they, really?" I asked.

"POE!" Anders shouted.

The hollows of his eyes were smeared with bootblack from the previous night's show, and remnants of corpse paint ribboned his hairline. He glared at me and pounded the table with his pudgy fist. Sid and Max soon joined in, pounding and shouting—"POE! POE! POE!"—and demanding I stop being such a pussy and chug my Potion of Evil.

The Rogue shakeup had made the consumption of THC a bit iffy, though. Rumors swirled about a drug test at the upcoming orientation at company headquarters down in Newport. While Rogue's marketing strategy appealed to the same well-worn revolutionary attitude that inspired the Green Dragon (see Rogue's "Declaration of Interdependence" which replaces the prose of Thomas Jefferson with sophomoric puns and scatology), the company ran its pubs by the book. Word around the taps was the new boss planned to clean house, with requisite urinalysis being a surefire way to cull the countercultural ranks.

I asked the band if they were worried about pissing hot.

"Nah," Sid said. "This stuff gets out of your system pretty fast."

"Totalitarians ain't gonna run my life," Anders said.

"I still can't believe those Republicans stole our bar," Max said.

≈

Those colonial revolutionary icons Rogue and the Green Dragon used to sell beer were from back east, but the West Coast bred the revolutionaries of the centuries to come.

Take Oregon's own Ken Kesey, who found inspiration in the Beats and flew over the cuckoo's nest only to land down in La Honda, California, where he and the Merry Pranksters painted an old school bus in Day-Glo and kick-started the Acid Generation, which a few years later would bloom into the hippie movement's rebellion against a proxy war that fed working-class kids into the military–industrial complex like so much fresh pink hamburger.

But just like LSD and Flower Power were ultimately no match for corporate greed and jingoism, craft beer has not usurped Big Beer, and now that conglomerates like AB-InBev and MillerCoors are buying up successful craft breweries, mainstreaming them, and thereby filling the shelves of every Safeway and Citgo in the nation with the same five or six brands, it's possible the artisanal beer movement has run up against a rampart that cannot be breached. There's only so much shelf space, after all, and more and more of the craft beer sold is simply generating profits for Big Beer, which will in turn be used to buy up still more upstart craft breweries and make sure they don't do anything *too* revolutionary. Seen in this light, craft beer was never going to prevail over Budweiser and Heineken any more than the hippies were going to stop Lockheed Martin from getting rich building and selling machines that kill people.

Depressing stuff, I suppose—unless our timeline is out of order.

First, consider that beer should be understood in the context of history, as it predates most everything we think of as historical. Beer emerged congruently with the agricultural revolution in the Fertile Crescent, which means that beer was around before printed literature, before medical science, before the wheel, and before most everything we think of as civilization. Even a macrobrew like Budweiser can trace its roots back to this honorable heritage, as Bud's original recipe was based on a beer produced by monks in a mountainous region of today's Czech Republic. So, it's all the more striking that Prohibition, which lasted just thirteen years, was able to erase nearly all the richness of that inherited history. In fact, the Big Beer-dominated era following repeal can be compared to the Dark Ages, as that period saw the repression of those humanist ideas that had flowered in the Classical Era much as Prohibition repressed the artfulness of the melting-pot beer culture that preceded it.

But if we continue along this line, we next reach the period that marks the end of the Dark Ages—the Renaissance—which suggests, perhaps, that by speaking of a craft beer *revolution* we are employing a colorful but ultimately inaccurate term.

The analogy isn't quite perfect. The Renaissance began in Italy before spreading throughout Europe, with Italians being primarily wine-drinkers— but what's ultimately important here is to note the revival of art and culture, of humanism and independent inquiry, and that spirit of geographical and spiritual exploration that'd been lost in the superstitious and clergy-dominated centuries that came before. And while the Renaissance nurtured those immortal artists whose names every schoolkid can rattle off, around the same time it produced a man in German ale country who was to make history in a different way.

This man, the reformer Martin Luther—in addition to defying Roman Catholic dogma and translating the New Testament for the common folk—once proclaimed: "Beer is made by men, wine by God." Although this may seem to malign beer, seen in another light it encapsulates perfectly the secular spirit of the Enlightenment that the Reformation helped usher into being. Because beer *is* made by men (and women). It's not providential, but a product. Beer has been with us since the birth of civilization, and thus its quality and character—or in the case of twentieth-century America, its lack thereof—is a reliable indicator of our cultural well-being.

This raises yet another question, though: who then is our modern-day Martin Luther of craft beer? Who, in other words, is the brave reformer who said enough to the powers that be and tore away the blinders, thereby allowing people to unshackle themselves from dogma and embrace the full flavor of humanism?

Come orientation day, I piled into a little car with Sabrina Pepper, Max, the reiki waitress, and a few others. The long and cramped drive was made worse by a collective grumpiness. While marijuana proponents argue the substance isn't addictive, anyone who doubts it's psychologically habit-forming is welcome to spend three hours ass-to-elbow with a gaggle of restaurant employees who haven't smoked in weeks after waking-and-baking for years.

The grumbling snowballed as we passed through McMinnville and the Willamette Valley, and the moaning increased as we caught Highway 18 to the coast. This continued all the way down scenic 101, past rocky shoreline and beaches framed by windbent pine and cedar, through the cheesy motels and seafood shacks of Lincoln City, then past Boiler Bay and onward to Otter Rock and Cape Foulweather, a cliffside promontory hundreds of feet above the Pacific named by James Cook in 1778 as he peered through the howling wind and rain.

Finally, we made fog-shrouded Newport herself. But after we'd circled down to the brewery on Yaquina Bay, the folks at Rogue Ales didn't seem as interested in testing our urine as they did in simply eyeballing the road-weary weirdos from Portland.

It's tempting to attribute America's beer reformation to one of the well-known early West Coast brewers, someone like Fritz Maytag of Anchor Steam, or Jack McAuliffe of New Albion, both of whom inspired the Widmer Brothers and other Northwest craft beer icons. But those guys are actually more akin to artists or skilled craftsmen: they're the Dante or Boccaccio figures, the Da Vinci or the Rembrandt. And though the foregoing comparisons were made with tongue planted firmly in cheek, these brewers nonetheless succeeded in reviving the poetics and sense of worldly perspective American beer had been missing in its medieval period, an individual and idiosyncratic voice on the page and the necessary vanishing point in landscape.

In the political and social sense, however, the true reformer was none other than the aforementioned Jimmy Carter. Because just like after Luther there was the Catholic Church but also Protestantism, which made way for various interpretations of Christ's teaching, after Carter there was Big Beer but also this mysterious thing called microbrew, which gave beer drinkers back the freedom to decide for themselves what was truly of value.

This suggests something else, too. Because if our new timeline is accurate and President Carter's 1979 legislation marks the reformation of craft beer, then that would mean we're only now entering America's Beer Enlightenment. And if that's the case, then it follows that the half-baked colonial era marketing schemes of both the Green Dragon and Rogue Ales were (are) getting ahead of themselves, and also that the eventual social and political revolutions Enlightenment ideas inspired in both Europe and the New World are yet to come.

≈

All this waxing philosophical about beer may strike some readers as a stretch, but craft beer really does mean a lot to people—to Portlanders, especially—and anxiety about its degradation fueled the animosity toward Rogue's takeover of the Green Dragon. Rogue charges a little more than average and, combined with gimmicky marketing ploys like the Declaration of Interdependence, the skepticism was thick as milk stout. Most of the Dragon's regulars were old enough to recall beer's homogenous dark ages, and many of them, rightly or wrongly, sensed in Rogue Ales the same bottom-line orientation that led to corporate America's assimilation and dilution of her priceless immigrant beer traditions.

Once down in Newport, though, Rogue didn't seem all that nefarious.

The day started with a tour of the brewing process: malting and milling, boiling wort and pitching yeast, conditioning and bottling and all of it filtered through the story of Rogue Ales. Our guide emphasized how different and independent the company was, painting Rogue as the feisty underdog, the rebel thumbing its nose at Big Beer. The speech felt a little forced, though, as if the company was trying to convince its newest employees of something it wasn't quite so sure of itself anymore. But the Dragon's crew had more pressing worries.

"When do you think they'll make us piss?" Max asked me.

Following the tour, we'd been served a complimentary lunch in the little bar overlooking the bay. Max and I both ordered what purported to be Kobe beef cheeseburgers.

"Forget about that," I said. "We've got free Kobe burgers."

"These things taste like freezer-burned hockey pucks," Max said.

"Such are the perks of corporate life," I said.

But Max was too nervous to eat. Instead, he drank his lunch—Dead Guy Ale, Rogue's flagship Maibock. Dead Guy's label is catchy: a grinning skeleton raises a frothy pint while perched atop a wooden keg. The hopheads in Portland may have been loath to admit it, but Rogue makes really good beer. In fact, we'd been given coupons for pints on the house. Having used both of mine already, I asked Sabrina Pepper for hers, as she apparently wasn't drinking.

"They're watching us," she whispered, "to see if you guys are dumb enough to drink on the clock."

I assured her I was plenty dumb enough. Max said he was dumb enough, too.

"There are cameras everywhere," she said.

When I asked if she really believed Rogue had brought us all the way down to Newport for a sting, she finally handed over the coupons, although not without a disapproving look.

This was rank paranoia, of course. Rogue was perfectly happy to comp a few lunchtime brews. All things considered, though, was the skepticism fair? Was it reasonable to lump Rogue Ales in with the likes of Big Beer—was the menace and machination the old guard perceived real, or the byproduct of a paranoid collective imagination?

Either way, what feels significant now is that the Green Dragon loyalists saw in their bar a place where money wasn't always the most important consideration. A place where a person might enjoy craft beer, sure, but more so enjoy an environment that's rare in modern America: one tuned to the needs of artfulness, and not just commerce.

Of course, the original Dragon failed exactly because it wasn't making enough money. So, perhaps I'm romanticizing the situation unduly? Nevertheless, I still can't help but admire those people, doomed as they so clearly are, who allow themselves to believe—despite all the evidence to the contrary—that genuine authenticity can somehow survive our culture's bottom line.

~~

Later that afternoon, orientation finished, we found ourselves outside in the parking lot once again. But Sabrina Pepper wasn't satisfied. "What about our goddamn pee test?" she said.

Max hocked up something in his throat. "If Rogue thinks I'm driving all the way back down here again without smoking a bowl"—he spat—"they're off their fucking rockers."

Then the reiki-practitioner's eyes widened, and she suggested we might've already *been* drug-tested. "I mean, how can we be sure they didn't, like, collect samples? From our silverware at lunch . . . or from the glasses we drank out of. Maybe that's why they gave us those beer coupons in the first place . . ."

The conversation continued in this vein for some time. But my coworkers hadn't cleansed their systems of their favorite metabolites and traveled all the way to Newport only for no resolution. Thus, after a hasty vote was taken, the crew marched straight back into Rogue's human resources office and demanded thorough and immediate urinalysis.

A kindly older woman glanced up from her ledgers. "I wasn't told about any . . . requirement like that."

"That's why the suits sent us down here," Max said.

"For orientation?"

"No, lady. To make sure we pissed clean."

When the befuddled woman asked who exactly had told us this testing was parcel to our employment, my coworkers gawped. "Everybody!"

Undeterred, we piled into the little car and drove to a nearby clinic. The place was closing for the day, but Sabrina and Max explained the situation to the bemused lab staff, and soon paperwork and paper cups were being filled out and up.

Feeling a little hesitant to thrust unsolicited urine upon total strangers, I took a walk down Bay Boulevard. The air was soupy with brine. A fog bank crept up the dampened street, Newport's rinky-dink trinket shops and chowder houses fading to white. The fog seemed to amplify sound: the sea sucking and rolling the shoreline rocks; a pelican's hoarse croak; the rubbery barks of sea lions lounging beneath the dock in a pile of warm brown blubber. Far out in the murk, a light pulsed. Then a plaintive horn sounded—a schooner home with the day's catch packed on ice, the boatmen hungry for a steaming bowl of chowder and a pint of Rogue's rich, malty brew.

During the takeover, Rogue had assured the beer community their acquisition of the Green Dragon was merely an effort to save a beloved taphouse by injecting some much-needed capital. And for eight years they were true to their word. Late in 2016, though, many years after I'd moved on, the company slayed the Dragon and rebranded it under their own name. In the interim, they got rid of the stage (and thus the live music), changed the menu to their standard pub fare, tore out the Quonset hut to expand outdoor seating, and installed thirty or so taps of their own beer as well as a pilot brewery. While some of these changes are arguably improvements, many in the community now see Rogue Ales—if you'll forgive one last colonial reference—as the craft beer equivalent of Benedict Arnold.

So, does the demise of the Green Dragon suggest the craft beer renaissance and enlightenment may not ultimately lead to those promised revolutions, after all? Will corporatism win yet another battle in the culture war? Because while Ken Kesey and the Pranksters left their mark, and a big chunk of the sixties' youth came to believe the robber barons and greedheads weren't going to win in the end—win they most certainly did. The hippies gave up or became bankers, Kesey got tossed in jail, and Hunter Thompson found himself compelled to write that melancholy line in *Fear and Loathing in Las Vegas* (1971) about how if you stand on a hill and look west you can almost see where the wave of idealism broke and rolled back.

And yes, our craft beer Martin Luther was run out of office by a Hollywood cowboy spouting feel-good lies about trickle-down economics, and the optimism and decency of the Obama years gave way to the hatemongering presidency of an amoral billionaire who nakedly schemes to loot the public trust and sack whatever is left of the American Dream. But disheartening as all of that may be, it doesn't necessarily mean the good ideas are dead, at least no more than classical notions of humanism and free thought were dead during the Dark Ages. Endangered, yes, and surrounded on all sides by ruthless enemies. But not dead. At least not yet.

8
IN PRAISE OF FOUR LOKO:
MOONLIGHTING IN THE LAND
OF ENCHANTMENT

Like many before me, I went to the desert hoping to change my life.

A change seemed in order, too, considering it'd now been five long years since I'd managed to parlay that law degree into the string of random bar gigs that constitute the backbone of this inauspiciously boozy narrative. Looking back at the lost young guy I was, though, his rootless lifestyle arose from a place I can sympathize with: in part, a desire to explore the country, to see and experience the unknown, but perhaps more so to the siren call of literature, that famous despoiler of all things steady and practical. It's easier to be a writer with no permanent address, after all, because that way the rejection never quite catches up with you.

But between the late nights and hungover mornings ("Drunkenness is temporary suicide," or so claimed Bertrand Russell, who must've tended bar at some point), I wasn't getting very much actual writing done. Or at least not much good writing. I had begun, struggled with, and ultimately abandoned two novels by this point. And to be clear, those were *terrible* novels. Faced with these facts, it occurred to me that I might benefit from a little wise counsel. So, I clipped out and polished up those parts of the novels that weren't quite so terrible and used them as evidence of seriousness in my application to a graduate fine arts program in New Mexico. Amazingly enough, I was accepted. Hopes rejuvenated, I swore an oath to change my ways, to put writing first and drinking second— and also to stay safely on the civilian side of the oak.

On my way there, however, I found my resolve quickly tested while visiting a series of thirsty old friends in the Bay Area and Southern California. By the time I hit I-8 east, my eyeballs felt packed in cotton, goldfish swam laps in my belly, and my breath was reminiscent of the kitty litter belonging to the dapper little fellow on the seat beside me. Sure enough, that morning I'd awoken to my trusty feline traveling companion, Bart—having finally managed to retrieve him from

L. A.—licking the tip of my nose and worriedly pawing my throat, as if checking for vitals.

Bart's concern was understandable, though, as mine was a hangover of such utter and skull-pounding grotesquery as to make one reconsider Thoreau's dictum that water is the only drink for a wise man. Nevertheless, as the miles slid past and the sun baked the booze from my system, I felt a little better. That, and I had something to look forward to—grad school in the Land of Enchantment. The desert has always been a place for seekers, and so going there to study writing made sense. But I had to actually get there first, and at a checkpoint near Yuma, Arizona, I found myself subject to a grilling by agents of the US Border Patrol.

A martial goon leaned into my window, breathed a scalding miasma of spearmint mouthwash in my face, and asked permission to search my vehicle.

When I scoffed and asked on what grounds, the agent answered like a typical fascist: with a question. "Sir, are you saying you don't want us to search your vehicle?"

I clarified that I merely wanted to know *why* he wanted to. Keep in mind it was ninety-nine windless degrees and the Honda's A/C hadn't worked since the presidency was stolen from Al Gore. While chewing over my reply, the officer hooked his thumbs in a shiny black leather belt, better to accentuate the unctuously gleaming handgun on his hip.

"Seems suspicious," he finally said.

Then a glut of legalese floated up to my lips from the bowels of my hangover, as if to prove the validity of state-dependent learning, and I rebuffed him by explaining how it'd been thoroughly adjudicated that probable cause for search and seizure could not rightly be based on a citizen's refusal to grant consent to agents of the government, of which he most certainly counted as one.

"That so?" the officer said and ran his hand over his flattop haircut.

Feeling emboldened, I pointed out the rather obvious fact that if my refusal to consent itself justified the search, then logically he wouldn't need to ask my permission at all. "That'd be a sort of catch-22, wouldn't it, officer?"

But he merely stared, seeming baffled as to how exactly I'd failed to recognize my status as a disheveled and disreputable man driving a shitty car along the Southwest's premier drug corridor—with a scruffy black tomcat riding shotgun, no less. Moreover, why didn't I appreciate the discrepancy in our power dynamic: that Uncle Sam had seen fit to vest him with the right to detain me, strip me of my civil liberties, and (if luck would have it) shoot me?

After conferring with his Kevlar-vested pals, the officer ordered me to pull off past the checkpoint, kill my engine, and wait. Which I lawfully did for thirty scorching minutes, until Bart was panting and my seat was sweated through to the rusty coils. Finally, a different officer approached. Paunchy and going silver, he asked why I was sitting there alongside the highway.

"Sitting here? I've been detained, I—"

"It seems a little suspicious, don't you think?"

Stammering now, the face I saw reflected in the officer's mirrored shades was oily and shifty and, yes, distinctly criminal-looking. I objected that his partner had violated my constitutional rights. When he seemed unmoved by this, I felt it only fair to warn him that I'd gone to law school.

He took another look at my bald-tired Honda. "*You* are an attorney?"

I began to backtrack, but he cut me off. "So, you're being untruthful with me right now?"

Not knowing what else to say, I admitted to having had a little trouble with the bar exam.

"Trouble like you forgot where the exam was? Like you forgot to bring a pencil—or trouble like you forgot the answers?"

"Look, officer, I'm a writer." Then I pointed at my heat-struck companion. "Bart and I are just trying to get to New Mexico, to study and teach at the university there."

"So, Bart the cat is a writer, too?"

How quickly things can cease to go our way.

"Did Bart also attend law school?" the officer asked. "He have some trouble with the bar exam, as well?"

I closed my eyes and gripped the gummy steering wheel, waiting for the command to step out of the vehicle. Instead, the officer double-tapped the Honda's roof and shooed me off down the road toward New Mexico with a gift I wouldn't recognize until years later: grist for the mill.

～

The village of Mesilla was the sort of place where men wore Stetsons and drove pickups out of genuine utility. The narrow streets were drifted over with windblown sand, and the historic square was lined with timeworn adobes with swamp coolers churning and dripping in their ceilings. Most of these buildings also featured plaques pertaining to Billy the Kid: the trinket shop claimed he was tried for murder there; the coffee shop said he escaped hanging there; while the bookstore suggested he just may have duped Pat Garrett there, and so on.

One such building—formerly the law offices of Col. Albert Jennings Fountain, who in 1881 unsuccessfully defended William H. Bonney on murder charges (although the Kid later escaped from jail, or so said a plaque across the plaza)—now housed a watering hole known as El Patio. No mere *bar*, El Patio was Mesilla's spiritual gathering place: a festering pit of characters frequented by students and musicians and working men (and the occasional working girl up from Ciudad Juarez), and a notorious local motorcycle gang for whom the thirsty crowd parted like water. It was faded and dusky inside, the juke a notch too loud, the pool cues warped, the urinals jammed with mesquite trimmings to help mask the stench.

Despite the sober oaths I'd sworn—which were not unlike the oaths I'd sworn upon leaving Ocean Beach for Jenny Lake—it was love at first sight. El Patio and I were inseparable, the relationship passionate, poisonous, and wholly symbiotic. I'd come to the desert for solitude, come like the third-century Desert Fathers seeking ascetic freedom—but, truth be told, I was a hardcore barfly. I graded student essays at El Patio during the day and spent evenings there, as well, bloviating with my fellow writers over icy cans of Tecate and warm, fat shots of Hornitos.

"Cormac McCarthy's self-conscious prosody," one of us well might've said, "is so clearly *not* the equal to Faulkner's idiom in Yoknapatawpha County. Jesus, are you drunk?"

"All this reflects nothing but the elitism of the White Guy Club," chimed in the female poet, before rolling another American Spirit and cracking her thumb joints.

"Realist literary fiction is dead anyway," said the writer who wore comic book T-shirts.

"The king is dead, long live the king," said the writer of realist literary fiction.

"If anybody sees a dancing bear," said the middle-aged and frighteningly alcoholic writer who may or may not have graduated a few semesters back, "I'm outta here."

Teaching English and drinking tequila didn't pay very well, though, and considering I spent most every night in a bar anyway, it made sense to do so on the clock. Part of me missed the life, too. The hustle, the wildness, the sweaty wads of cash. El Patio wasn't hiring, unfortunately, but I soon landed at a nearby country club. While it wasn't really my scene—I hate golf and distrust the rich— there was one member whom I came to know pretty well.

Elliot Santiago lived with his mother in a luxury home just off the fourth tee. He was Hispanic and in his mid-fifties, short and yappy and dripping sarcasm. He wore embroidered western shirts with pearl buttons, along with a pair of bejeweled white leather cowboy boots the toes of which rolled up into stylish (if somewhat leprechaunish) curlicues. Elliot had a bitchy reputation—most staff avoided him—but considering he never talked about golf, he was soon my favorite bar patron. He ran a catering company, providing both ritzy events for the local bourgeoisie ("I hate this fucking retirement home," he said of the country club, "but it's good for business"), as well as meals for the county halfway house. In fact, he made a point of offering the ex-cons jobs. Most of them weren't actually bad people, he explained, just fuckups.

Elliot also disliked Jeff, the bar manager. Jeff was one of those basically clueless guys who find themselves in the industry for life and—instead of declaring himself one of the world's great undiscovered artists, or at least honorably commencing to drink in earnest—go back to school for a degree in restaurant management. Whatever else Jeff may have learned, he'd aced the section on passing the buck, and being low man on the putter meant that I often found myself cleaning hairy goop from under the coolers and lugging around cases of booze, all while Jeff stood idly by and critiqued my efforts. So, I appreciated that Elliot gave him a hard time.

One night in particular stands out. Elliot had come in for a few vodka-cranberries and Jeff was busy sucking up to him when Elliot—totally ignoring Jeff's chitter-chatter—dug into his pocket for his phone, only to yank his hand free and send a half-dozen little baggies of white powder raining down atop the bar and floor like cellophane-wrapped snowflakes.

"Fuck!" Elliot snapped. "Jeff, pick that shit up."

Bug-eyed, Jeff looked my way. But I pretended to be absorbed in the Golf Channel.

"Get your ass over here right now, Jeff," Elliot said, "and pick up my fucking cocaine."

Other members had noticed by now; forkfuls of beef wellington hung dripping in the pregnant air. Finally, Jeff came around the bar and quietly gathered the spilled baggies before returning them to Elliot. Then he scurried into the general manager's office to complain. But this manager—a man who I once witnessed dump half a bottle of Macallan into a Big Gulp for his drive home—calmly explained that nobody wanted to hear ugly rumors like that.

Before Elliot left that night, he asked how much I made at the club. Figuring the question was harmless enough, I gave him a ballpark figure. "Quit wasting your time," he said, and promised to pay me double.

I asked if I'd be expected to pick up his fucking cocaine for him.

"I'm decorating a breast cancer benefit this weekend," he said. "I'll pay you a hundred bucks just to haul some pink shit around for a couple hours."

Pink shit?

"Fine," he said, seeing my hesitation, "make it two-hundred."

I asked if he was serious, because two-hundred dollars for a few hours of work sounds awfully good to a broke student—if not a little too good to be true.

"Trust me," Elliot said, "those cougars are gonna love you."

≈

Since coming to New Mexico, I was spending more time than ever in bars. Much as with that summer in the Tetons, I'd wanted to change my life, temper my intemperate habits, and focus on writing and literature. And here was another chance, yet I found myself constantly pulled back to the bar—to both sides of it—as if by some perverse gravity.

Working for Elliot proved interesting, though. In fact, hauling pink shit to the fundraiser was just the beginning. After schmoozing his clients, Elliot dragged me outside and said, "Check out the party wagon."

He'd rented a sixteen-passenger van with the intention of showing a group of wealthy local housewives a good time. He tossed me the keys and told me to crank up the radio. "Play something peppy," he said, "to counteract all the Xanax these chicks have to pop to stay married to their limp-dick husbands."

And that's how I found myself driving a posse of ladies to one backyard soiree after another, from hotel lounge to honky-tonk and finally to a biker bar out in the middle of the desert that made El Patio look like the Rainbow Room. Prior to departure, we'd outfitted the van with a few magnums of chardonnay, a ream of red plastic cups, and (presumably as a joke) a case of Four Loko, a beverage then popular with the college crowd. In fact, the stuff had made headlines ("blackout in a can") after nine students from Central Washington University were hospitalized upon consuming too much of it. The brightly towering cans may have looked like soft drinks, but Four Loko boasted upwards of 12 percent industrial malt liquor and massive amounts of stimulant: not just caffeine but guarana, an Amazonian climbing plant packing two to three times the punch of coffee, as well as taurine, a mysterious hormone-rich jelly culled from the amygdalae of extraterrestrials recovered at UFO crash sites near Roswell.

The FDA eventually caught wind and put the kibosh on the uppers (nothing gold can stay, as Frost reminds us) but that night the ladies got thoroughly Loko, soaring high on mango-berry and taurine-infused wings.

Clearly pleased with himself, Elliot crouched between the van's front seats and whispered under his wine-tinted breath. "I'm telling you, hobnobbing's the name of the game."

"It's not really my style," I said, "but thanks for having me along."

"What do you mean it's not your style? You're a fucking *bartender.*"

When I reminded Elliot I was also a writer, he frowned. So, I explained (for the fourth or fifth time since we'd met) the creative writing program and my teaching assistantship.

"I thought you were joking about that shit," he said.

When I failed to respond, he continued. "Listen up, Lurch, you need to forget the books and figure out how to fleece the jet-set." We hit a bump and he spilled chardonnay all over the console. "Believe me, kissing these cougars' bleached assholes still beats working for a living."

And Elliot seemingly had a point, because if this was work it was work of an unusual sort. The van was really rocking. Perhaps the sheer trashiness of Four Loko had transported those impeccably groomed women back to the halcyon days of the early nineties, when crow's feet had belonged only to the birds and tribal script lumbar tattoos acquired during Acapulco spring break constituted not shortsighted decision-making, but liberating statements of nonconformity, a time when they'd been happier and freer and less worried about floundering marriages and flexible mortgages and the interminable social obligations of that crusty old country club.

The night was far from over, though. In fact, moments later I was busy piloting the van under the looming pecan trees when a pair of perfumed arms suddenly embraced me. Teased hair tickled my cheek and saccharine breath bathed my face. Then we hit a bump and the woman grabbed me, popping buttons off my shirt. Barely keeping the boxy van between the lines, I called out to Elliot for assistance, but he was busy telling off-color jokes in the back.

The woman slurred a stream of garbled and vaguely lewd innuendo into my ear, before revealing that Elliot had told her and the other girls *all* about me. Then one of her friends demanded to know just what exactly I thought I was being paid for, while another laughed and said I needed to stop playing coy, while yet another woman demanded to know how a guy who did *that* for a living could be such a wallflower?

"Quiet, bitches!" Elliot shouted.

But the perfumed woman still pawed at me, rooting around inside my shirt while mumbling sour nothings in my ear. I rode the brakes, imagining us careening into an arroyo, cans of Four Loko and loose sequins flying from the busted windows, laughter turned screaming, detention and booking and the shame of having to face my students after they'd all seen my mugshot in the *Las Cruces Sun-News*.

Then I fell victim to a wet and popping hickie.

All the while, Elliot demanded in the shrillest of tones that his client cease her molestations and unhand the handsome young chauffeur right this fucking instant—although a glance in the rearview revealed him laughing and egging her on, stomping his curly boots and waving his hands about like a miniature conductor / satyr.

I like to think I drove pretty well that night, all things considered. Until my inamorata's tongue slithered down the old ear canal, that is. Badly startled, I mashed the brakes and the van skidded off-road and down into a shallow ditch. Everybody yelped and whooped, and sugary malt liquor splashed the seats and carpet. In the stillness to follow, our headlights burned twin holes in the moonless desert night and a rooster tail of opalescent dust curtained the steaming hood.

Then the engine ticked and coughed, and the cougars roared, and Elliot flashed his big, capped teeth and—almost like an afterthought—pulled two crisp hundred dollar bills from his wallet and stuffed them in my shirt pocket.

"You're welcome," he said.

≈

Not long after the fundraiser, Elliot's number popped up on my phone.

I hesitated to answer but when I finally did, he launched into a story about this hoity-toity wedding he'd agreed to cater near the village of Hatch. He needed a tall, Anglo bartender, he said, to make the operation seem legit. How'd two-hundred more bucks sound?

But I had misgivings, and they were threefold: first, I suspected my classmates would be spending the weekend at home, snuggled up with their laptops; second, I'd made exactly zero progress in my nonfiction workshop because I *still* couldn't think of anything to write about; and finally, a juicy rumor had spread rather mysteriously among the country club housewives, the upshot being that

Elliot's newest assistant moonlighted not only as a bartender and van driver, but as a dildo model.

Be all of that as it may, come the weekend I found myself decked out in black slacks, shiny shoes, and a crisp white shirt. The bed and breakfast sat in a valley ringed by cotton fields, the dirt roads lined with cypresses. I helped Elliot lug his equipment into a hearth-like kitchen beyond which lay an atrium with a burbling stone fountain and citrus trees strung with lights. The owners were a pair of eccentric California refugees who obviously adored Elliot, indulging his caustic humor and fawning over his event-planning expertise.

After setting up the bar under a sprawling live oak, I met my coworkers. Turns out Elliot had hired seemingly every perky young woman in southern New Mexico, and he'd poured them all into slinky black dresses. But he'd also hired one guy who wasn't quite so perky. Shaven-headed and wolfish, he stalked around while tugging at the starched collar of the shirt Elliot had obviously provided. Up close, a teardrop was inked blue on his weather-beaten cheekbone.

As the festivities got under way, Elliot morphed into a blur of stress and began screaming outrageously at any employee foolish enough to veer too close. Those high-heeled cocktail waitresses turned dainty little ankles in their haste to escape this mincing madman suddenly barking orders and cussing them for lazy trollops. Whatever happened to nice Mr. Elliot? Who was this Nazi in the pink shirt and curly-toed boots?

Later, Elliot caught me holding a bottle of chardonnay around the middle and not by the punt, as proper service etiquette dictates. Wearing a gracious smile for the unsuspecting guests, Elliot hissed in my ear (or as close to my ear as his height allowed), "Were you raised in a *cave*? Pour from the punt— from the fucking punt!" Then he hid behind me and poured himself a glass, so the wedding party wouldn't see him guzzling the wine they'd already paid for. I glanced over my shoulder and said the wine was pretty decent, especially considering it was local.

"Wine is like everything else in New Mexico," Elliot said, "the whiter the better."

"It's buttery," I said, "but not cloying."

"Five bucks a bottle," Elliot said, "wholesale."

"A love song to grapefruit delicately tuned with oak."

"Like sweet beads of sweat," Elliot said, "licked from the peach fuzz on Zac Efron's—"

I tuned out the rest. Moments later, Elliot chased after a waitress struggling under a tray of braised shrimp. "Smile, goddamn it!" He slapped her on the ass. "Sway those hips! What the fuck do you think I'm paying you for?"

As the gig wore on, I poured more wine and made small talk and helped the waitresses with the heftier trays of hors d'oeuvres, but I found myself distracted. My mind kept returning to an essay I'd recently read by the prolific and polymathic Bertrand Russell—"In Praise of Idleness"—wherein he argues against the ethos of hard work. He suggests that more leisure is necessary to truly enjoy life, and the assumption that working people require or deserve less of it is simple classist prejudice. In fact, after reading his polemic, Russell hopes "the leaders of the YMCA will start a campaign to induce good young men to do nothing."

Similarly, Thoreau (in addition to wisely drinking his water) writes how the laboring man has difficulty appreciating culture, not because his mind is coarse, but because paying attention to anything other than his labor depreciates his market value, which is all society rewards him to think about. Like Russell, Thoreau believes our innermost natures will shrivel if ignored or roughly handled. "Yet we do not treat ourselves," he writes, "nor one another thus tenderly."

Being both an aspiring writer and a laboring man (of a sort), I was inclined to agree. People do need more free time to think and learn and express themselves. But then why did I feel compelled to spend so much of my free time slinging drinks? Because it wasn't just the money. No, I *needed* to bartend. An entire weekend spent reading on the couch? An evening of nothing but sketching my thoughts in a journal? Taking a long walk—not to El Patio, but simply to meditate on the trees and sky? These were things I'd felt sure I wanted prior to coming to the desert—things I still did want—and yet I wasn't doing them. In fact, I was doing everything in my power not to do them.

But why? What was stopping me from taking advantage of this opportunity?

Part of it was that, after years of dutifully plowing through the literary canon in my scant free time, fiction had somehow begun to seem less compelling than the everyday people and situations I encountered behind the bar. Take, for example, the intriguing woman in the rose-red dress who walked up just then and asked me for a glass of cabernet.

"Preferably Napa," she said.

"Sorry, but I'm pouring only the finest terroir of the Great Chihuahuan Desert."

This earned me a smile. "New Mexican wine tastes like Kool-Aid," she said.

I poured her a glass anyway, and we got to talking, pausing whenever I had to uncork a fresh bottle or go convince Elliot not to fire all the waitresses. Turns out, the woman was a journalist on a freelance assignment. Another writer—a pretty one in a red dress? Figuring nobody ought to drink alone, I took a cue from my boss and poured myself some clandestine wine.

A bit later, we were deep into a discussion of the virtues of the nineteenth-century novel—the Kool-Aid tasting better and better—when Teardrop appeared at the bar. He just stood there, wordlessly gnashing his raw lips. Then he cranked his head around and shot an electric glare at Elliot, who was across the courtyard glad-handing the father of the bride. Finally, I realized what was so unsettling about Teardrop's appearance. It wasn't just the jailhouse facial tattoo and the twitchiness; it was how the whites of his eyes shown all the way around, like in *A Clockwork Orange* when they pin the recidivist's lids open and force him to watch grisly films.

I asked if everything was okay.

"I gonna rip that little *cabrón* a new asshole," Teardrop said, "and watch him bleed."

The journalist gasped; I nearly spat out my wine.

"He *cursed* me, vato. Nobody curse at me and just walk away."

I tried my best to assure Teardrop that Elliot hadn't really meant whatever he'd said.

"All I did was spill some water on his . . . rag things."

Then I understood what must've happened. Elliot had a collection of silk doilies he expended much care arranging at his events, getting the color combination, the texture and flow, just right. His first love was design, and he had a good eye, but Elliot could be oversensitive—and less than diplomatic—should a careless employee compromise his aesthetics. I was in the midst of explaining all this when Teardrop interrupted.

"I will not be talked to that way," he said. "I am not his son."

Palms up, I gave a pacifying smile. "Just wait," I said. "In five minutes Elliot will forget all about it. He'll probably give you a beer."

Then Teardrop glared at me with those bulging eyes and explained in no uncertain terms that he could not—could no longer—drink any form of alcohol, not even a single beer.

Not knowing what else to say, I offered to pour him a Coca-Cola.

"No man judge me but God," he said.

Combined with the eerie stillness of Teardrop's face, this unnerving reply left me at a loss. I briefly considered appealing to his macho ego (no real tough guy would bother roughing up a little twerp like Elliot, right?) or maybe his sense of fair play (after all, the job Elliot had given him did fulfill a condition of his parole)—but then my companion intervened.

"When silk gets wet it turns darker," the journalist said. She gave Teardrop a motherly smile. "And that can spoil the color scheme. Your boss just wants everything to look nice."

Her feminine presence seemed to call him back from the edge.

"Just let it slide," I said. "Seriously. Elliot thinks you're doing a terrific job."

Teardrop looked me hard in the face and asked if Elliot had really said this about him, and I promised he most certainly had. Furthermore, I assured him that Elliot was proud of him, proud he was holding down a job and living sober. Teardrop listened intently to these words—almost too intently. But just when I felt sure he was about to punch my lying jaw, the blue tear trembled on his cheek as if the ink were wriggling up from the depths of his skin.

"No one has ever said that to me before," he admitted, and then he jammed his hands in his pockets and returned to the table where Elliot had stationed him.

Relieved, I was about to pour more wine for the journalist when she took hold of my wrist. "Oh my goodness, look . . ."

Amidst the bustle of the reception, Teardrop had taken a knee and begun blotting Elliot's doilies with a clean white towel. He fussed over each one, patting them dry, careful not to disturb the lay of the fabric. My companion leaned against me, watching him, and I could still feel her there flush to my ribs after she stepped away. A moment later, a creosote-rich gust rivered through the live oak and leaves pinwheeled down amongst the crates of wine and icy beer.

Across the yard, Teardrop pursed his chapped lips and blew on the gossamer silk.

≈

Hemingway, that famously alcoholic and womanizing 1954 Nobel Prize winner, once wrote that while experience tends to dull the finer sensibilities, he'd rather have to sharpen his talent on the old grindstone and whetstone than have nothing to say. On the other hand, Bertrand Russell—a lifelong teetotaler but, like Hemingway, also a husband to four wives and a 1950 Nobel Prize winner—argues the leisure class, "contributed nearly the whole of what we call civilization." He's thinking not only of the rich themselves, but of the tradition of patronage that has freed creative people to perform work of aesthetic or intellectual—but not necessarily monetary—value. It's those who don't have to haul bricks or shake cocktails all day who get to write the books. It's not that working folks aren't talented or motivated, it's that they're *tired*.

Still, while the bar life was undeniably tiring, I eventually came to accept that booze and late nights were parcel to my authentic experience in this realm, and if one wants to be a writer, he or she is obligated to explore such experience. But how?

I'd read the famous auteurs of drinking—Hunter Thompson's rum-fueled escapades; Bukowski slugging it out with a bottle of rotgut; Malcolm Lowry pickling himself in mezcal; Hemingway's constant ice-cold daiquiris (paid for by his increasingly wealthy string of wives)—and yet my own go-arounds with inebriation and the provision of it seemed comparatively mundane, not dripping with epiphany like the great stories by the great writers. I was also troubled by a sense that the bookish life I yearned for was actually just a fantasy. Throughout the years I'd bounced around tending bar, I'd privately thought of myself as a writer, and this had helped me deal with the drudgery. Whereas now that I'd come to the desert and was surrounded by writers, I felt more than ever like a masquerading bartender.

Regardless, I spent the years to follow buried to my neck in books—anytime I wasn't working catering gigs, that is, or tending the many bars that came later. The constant hustle denied me that idleness that Russell claims is indispensable for creative work (of note: Russell published over one hundred books and articles in his lifetime), and maybe that's why only a fraction of what I wrote during that period reached its full potential. But I did come to understand something I hadn't during my years in the desert, and that lesson—if I've not misconstrued it in my proletarian exhaustion—has to do with a necessary balance between the experiential and the intellectual, as vivid output often seems to require vivid inputs.

I'd thought I needed to escape my life, that somewhere out in the sand and wind and heat was a literary secret the bars and cocktails and cities were blinding me to—but this merely begs the question of what exactly I'd ever thought I would write about? Because now it seems to me that writers, wherever they live and whatever they have to do for money, either write or they don't; and Four Loko—the original kind, with all the speedy chemicals—is as good a muse as any, at least for those of us born without the luxury of idleness.

9

THE MACHINE IN OUR POCKET: DRINKING ALONE IN IPHONE WORLD

Back in 2007, when I'd first moved to Ocean Beach and begun serving up margaritas at Casa de Agave, when I first met Arturo and Bentley and all the rest of the crew, there came an otherwise unremarkable summer day when a young waiter named Caesar showed up with something entirely new. "Hey guys," he said, "check this out."

I'd thought it was just another phone, until I noticed the sophistication of the screen.

"It's called the iPhone," Caesar said, and then used two fingers to widen out the display so we could all get a better look.

"Those are all the rage in the tech mags," Bentley said. "Apple stock is blowing up."

"Great," Arturo said, eyeing it over the rim of his cocktail. "Now they'll expect me to file briefs while I'm here trying to enjoy whatever's left of my fading youth."

"You're such a Negative Nancy," Bentley said. "It's just a phone."

"That thing is no *phone*," Arturo said. "It's an electronic leash."

"Whatever. It's a tool, like a laptop but smaller. Email, porn, etcetera."

"Etcetera is right," Arturo said. "This is the final nail in the coffin—you'll see."

I bent closer to the silvery light spilling from the palm of Caesar's hand. He punched a link and the screen instantly resolved to a new page. The resolution was crisp, the colors vivid, the graphics sharp. Impressed, I commented that it must've been pretty expensive.

"Yeah, but so what?" Caesar said. "Just look at it—this shit is the future."

 ⁓

And so it was, although the years to come would see the world change in ways both incredible and fascinating, but also somewhat disturbing and difficult to fathom.

In 2013, for example, a university student was shot to death at random shortly after stepping off a crowded commuter train in San Francisco. Prior to the murder, security footage showed the assailant brandishing a handgun in plain sight, as if clamoring for the attention of his potential victims. He even paused to wipe his runny nose with the gun, but the passengers—a dozen of them—were all too engrossed in their smartphones and tablets to notice the homicidal madman in their midst.

More recently, it was reported that Silicon Valley tech workers have begun requiring nannies to sign detailed "no-phone contracts" meant to ensure their children will under no circumstances be exposed to screen time—an attempt, it would seem, to spare the progeny the addictive nature of the parent's life's work.

Examples like this could be piled up to the iCloud, of course—the impact of smartphones and vehicular crashes leaps instantly to mind—but beyond inattention to our physical safety and pitfalls for the developing brain are the emotional repercussions for the screen-addicted individual, as well as the philosophical ramifications for a world caught in the grip of a new sort of psychological or perhaps even spiritual disease, an epidemic of silence where connection (or the illusion of it) is the contagion and the prognosis is bleak.

Still, outside of extenuating circumstances—the speeding car, distraction in the face of a psychopath—this disease is not fatal. Instead, it's a lingering malady, like boils for the psyche. But unlike boils, this affliction cannot be lanced or covered up with long sleeves or miraculously relived at the behest of an Old Testament god. Instead, it settles deep inside of us and gnaws at the very root of our emotional balance: our comfort with solitude and inner silence.

In this vein (and though we'll keep bars and booze in mind), let's widen our frame of reference to consider the work of a painter and a philosopher from the century pre-smartphone.

≈

Much like Warhol's tomato soup cans or Dali's melting clocks or Wood's rural gothic, Edward Hopper's *Nighthawks* (1942) is one of a handful of twentieth-century paintings that exist in today's collective consciousness. You know Hopper's figures: they sit in the nighttime diner, no entrance or exit visible, sealed behind a plate glass window as if in a fishbowl, the light having an eerie aquatic-green quality. There's a businessman with his back to us, fedora low on his head, and across from him an identically dressed man and his date, a redhead in a red dress with downcast eyes. There's also a lone employee bent at some task, his hands out of sight under the counter. What unites these figures as they linger over their coffee and chores is a palpable reluctance to speak the simple words that would pierce the loneliness and ennui.

But while it's a melancholy scene, there's a sense in *Nighthawks* that the figures are aware of their condition. They've gathered after all, even if they do not quite speak or touch. And the diner is that quintessential well-lighted place. It's as if they're more comfortable being alone together, as if human solidarity might yet push back against the city's encroaching darkness. These are people who know what it is to be alone and silent and are navigating that psychic space as best they can. It's not unlike listening to a sad song when feeling blue. There's consolation in being alone together, a sense of community, an unspoken acknowledgment that we are all castaways aboard the same raft.

Now imagine if Hopper were around to paint this same diner scene today. See that lone businessman, the one with his back to us—he's bent low over the counter, posture broken and spine rounding. There's also a secondary source of light other than those ghostly fluorescents; the sliver of his cheek glows with it. And that second businessman and the woman in red—he's no longer holding a cigarette and she's no longer idly studying that matchbook. Instead, they're both hunched over their cupped hands. Their faces too are strangely aglow, as if lit by tiny blue gas flames, although their expressions are markedly different. That knowing and communal melancholy is gone, replaced by faint, placid smiles.

As for that lone employee, he's now standing up straight with his back turned to his customers. The grimace of effort is gone from his face, replaced by something not unlike serenity, and his hand hovers an inch above his apron pocket, his neck craned down at an unnatural angle as he peeks at the spill of light emanating from his palm.

≈

Just one year after *Nighthawks,* Jean-Paul Sartre published *Being and Nothingness,* which asks us to imagine a hypothetical café waiter—one perhaps not so different from Hopper's diner employee, or a bartender such as myself. By virtue of this example and others, Sartre lays out a number of concepts that feel relevant in our world of screens.

First, the idea of existence preceding essence, with this being an inherently meaningless world unless we manage to create the very authenticity our psyches crave. We show up on the scene first, in other words, and only then may we begin to define our purpose. Having found ourselves abandoned in a universe that's unaware of us and our needs, we inherit the crushing responsibility of living according to values of our own making. *Cogito ergo sum,* and so on.

We're not alone in this forlornness, however. While Sartre famously gave a character in *No Exit* the bombastic line, "Hell is other people!" he didn't necessarily mean it the way it sounds. Instead, other people constitute a chance to know ourselves, to see ourselves judged in the eyes of another thinking primate and thereby gain knowledge we'd otherwise have no access to. In this inescapably subjective world, the human condition does still seem to exist—we can be brilliant or foolish, liars or honest, craven or courageous—but it's only through the eyes of other people that we can truly know our own condition. We need each other in this way.

But this brings us around to the hell of iPhone World. Because one's state of being in the land of screens is predicated not upon knowledge of a shared human condition, but an illusion of connection. So long as our devices are glowing, we can keep on telling ourselves this creeping unease, this sense of being abandoned, isn't really the truth. No, while we may not authentically communicate in the present moment, we're happy enough following the doings of our friends on Facebook. We are consciously deciding to ignore the people around us—so much so that we cannot even bother to meet that café waiter's eyes when he comes to our table—but this isn't because we're rude; it's because we're texting a cousin, or we're updating our Instagram account with curated photos of the salad that same waiter served us for lunch.

Now such distraction might seem harmless enough, unless Sartre was right about other people. Because if the cogito only works in relation to others like itself, then living in a world where individuals are increasingly isolated and yet laboring under a delusion of connection seems dangerous—dangerous not only for emotional well-being, but for our ability to live authentic lives.

There are many (such as Bentley) who would say our screens are just tools, that these devices that have infiltrated every facet of human life aren't in fact so very different from a screwdriver or a pair of pliers. In this sense, just like reality as described by Sartre, our screens are without a priori good or evil. And while there may be some abstract truth in this, it's a truth predicated on bad faith. It's not unlike those who argue assault rifles are mere tools, in hopes of drowning out the sounds of bullets ricocheting off lockers in the hallways of our schools or clanging off the pavement at country music shows on the Vegas Strip.

Yes, I was born into that last generation who grew up in a world without screens, a world of paper books full of strange and wonderful characters the likes of which one might perchance someday meet, and paper maps depicting far-flung and exotic places one might someday see first-hand, and perhaps that was unlucky timing. We had Nintendo and HBO, but otherwise were stuck with telephones and the Encyclopedia Britannica. Most days I feel like a refugee, and the temptation to look back on my childhood as prelapsarian is embarrassingly strong. Because make no mistake, this is a brave new world, and new worlds require new ontologies.

Iungo ergo sum. I connect; therefore, I exist.

$$\approx$$

A decade after Caesar walked into Casa de Agave with that first generation smartphone, I found myself in an airport bar somewhere in Texas, looking to drink away a layover—but the bar was peculiar in that screens were mounted at each stool.

While I'd never encountered such a setup before, life in iPhone World had coded me to understand it intuitively. So, I commenced to navigate: first, a screen disambiguating beer, wine, spirits, or cocktails; then another (in my anxiety I'd chosen spirits) disambiguating vodka, gin, bourbon, scotch, or rum. I kept pushing buttons, changing my mind and starting over, until eventually an actual flesh-and-blood bartender materialized.

"Having some trouble?"

I glanced up. He was about my same age. I asked if people liked ordering their drinks this way.

"Some older folks are put off by it," he said, "but the young ones don't really seem to notice much difference."

Spooked, I asked him for a double Woodford, neat.

"Sure, but you'll still have to punch it in. I can't pour a drop until you do."

When I continued to hesitate, he leaned across the bar and performed the necessary motions for me, as if I were one of those fusty old folks. In the meantime, a glut of passengers had spilled onto the concourse, and one by one the stools filled. I glanced down the rail at all those strangers pecking at the glowing screens. Then they began pecking at other screens, the ones on their phones, the ones on their laptops, their pads and tablets and watches. I carried screens of my own by then, of course, but there's something about a bar, a reverent feeling I get whenever I belly up to one, which suggests a person really ought to leave those devices be.

Not so for my fellow travelers. Between all their screens, they were busier than if they'd still been at work, much as Arturo had predicted years before. The bartender was busy now, too—pouring wine, drawing beer, mixing gin-and-tonics—and while he delivered each drink to its corresponding stool-tablet with a professional smile, he barely spoke. *There you are,* or maybe just *Cheers* or *Enjoy.* But he wasn't being curt. Nor did the lack of conversation owe to the transitory nature of an airport lounge. No, this was something new: a hush of screens.

Bartender and customers alike had been rendered silent and strangely invisible to one another. Only I had actually been heard and seen, and this only due to my hesitation. As in the diner from *Nighthawks,* there was much melancholy here, but there was also something else—a collective solitude that wasn't possible in the past. A solitude born not of geography or an individual's reticence to speak and engage, but by the all-too-human desire for connection itself.

To help make sense of this paradox we might look back a century prior to Hopper and Sartre, to the life and words of America's greatest chronicler of solitude—Henry Thoreau—as well as a book by one of his farseeing critics.

≈

While Thoreau never worked as a café waiter, let alone a bartender ("I would fain keep sober always" he writes) those years of self-imposed isolation at Walden Pond gave us not only the admonition to simplify our lives, but the existential command to befriend our capacity for aloneness. It's wholesome to be alone, according to Thoreau, as too much interaction with other people grows wearisome. So, both a teetotaler and a hermit, yes, but a teetotaling hermit who understood himself at a depth most of us will never even sniff.

Although Thoreau had a healthy esteem for humanity, he felt that to live in the thick of society was to cheapen ourselves and lessen our respect for others. Without sufficient aloneness we haven't the necessary space to reflect and thereby become fuller and better people, and so when we again meet we can bring nothing new to the table.

He came to these conclusions when, compelled to venture into town, he would bump into acquaintances who inevitably asked whether he didn't get a tad lonesome living out in the woods all by himself. For Thoreau, however, the real question was "what sort of space" actually separates people in a harmful way. And if he was right, if we really do need time apart in order to better value our time together, what becomes of us in a world that's predicated on constant connection, or at least the unbroken simulacrum of it—if time alone has the power to better us, to provide us with insight and allow us to reflect upon and grow from experience, what sort of stagnation occurs when society is always present, chattering in the palm of your hand?

Still, Thoreau does admit to a time when he felt unpleasantly lonesome, when he worried that perhaps his foray into the woods wasn't so much an attempt to live deliberately and suck the marrow out of life, but just a nutty misstep. He's quickly bolstered in his resolve, however, by the friendly sound of pattering raindrops and the majesty of a neighboring tree scored tip to foot by lightning. Nature, in other words.

Again, though, the modern reader is left to wonder whether trees and thunderstorms can possibly compete with interactive screens, especially when those screens have divorced our senses so thoroughly from the very nature Thoreau took solace in. Along these lines, his description of his own solitude is worth considering. "I have," he writes, ". . . my own sun and moon and stars, and a little world all to myself."

A little world all to myself?

What is iPhone World if not a portable facsimile of the exact same conceit?

But in describing the treasured privacy he found in nature, Thoreau also notes something ominous—the distant view of a railroad—and around this potent symbol would coalesce the ideas of the critic Leo Marx, notably *The Machine in the Garden* (1964).

The book argues that American literature (and the nation in general) reflects a proverbial Fall from pastoral grace. According to Marx, America initially saw itself as an unspoiled garden, a new Eden, and the history of technological change and Manifest Destiny is the story of a people asserting dominion over nature. The machine, then, is the implacable force that penetrates and alters the pastoral landscape.

For Thoreau and other writers of his day, this meant the mechanization represented by the coming of the railroad and steam engine, whereas in the twentieth century it came to mean industrialization and urbanization more broadly, whereas in our current century it perhaps means something like an airport bar full of people with lowered heads who navigate screens in lieu of the messiness of navigating actual human interaction.

Marx is no Luddite, though. At the dawn of the industrial age, he points out that machines were widely hailed as the means by which people would emancipate their minds from their labor. Where once people had toiled dawn to dusk (such as Thoreau's forays into raising beans), now they might work indoors at tasks requiring less muscle and ultimately less time. And as technology grew more sophisticated, so would this math continue to favor ease of life. Believers in such progress, like Ralph Waldo Emerson (a friend and mentor to Thoreau, as well as a fellow teetotaler), saw in technology a liberating force; the new machines could only improve the lot of the human race, and just might bring about something like Thomas More's utopian vision of a day evenly split between practical work and fruitful leisure.

Progress rarely comes scot-free, however, and the machine in the garden is now the machine in our pocket, which really means the machine in our head, and the people who make these machines are so disturbed by the power of what they've done that they force their nannies to sign contracts prohibiting their children's exposure to them. And it may turn out that this caution is fully warranted, because if the goal of nineteenth-century mechanization was the liberation of the mind from mindless tasks, how best to sum up the goal of a twenty-first-century technology that seems to aim at the exact opposite: to control the attention span and make an addict of consciousness via the lulling illusion of constant connection.

Perhaps these reflections veer into Chicken Little territory, or maybe they're the sort of thing only that most outdated of persons—the writer, that absurdly antiquated devotee of paper-and-pen, that scribbler who doesn't even scribble in-real-time—would ever bother to worry about. But consider that, for all its ugliness, industrialization didn't exist on the scale of the individual; it was the proverbial locomotive of social change, something unmissable due to sheer volume and size, and thus it couldn't infiltrate the mind and spirit quite so surreptitiously. That other Marx's alienation, which might also be described as estrangement from the natural world, was easy enough to recognize. Not so for our screens.

In Thoreau's time, critics of mechanization worried it separated people from nature (and by extension human nature), but Thoreau himself clearly realized the industrial revolution was inevitable—although whether for good or ill he couldn't say. And so it is for today's screen revolution, the devices being woven as deeply into the social fabric as those railroad tracks were laid and spiked in that Massachusetts forest. Not a new means of production with the fallout of a scarred landscape, sooty trees, and smoke-filled skies, but an entirely new way of being, one with an eerie power to stroke the ego while quietly penetrating the id, and one that requires a weird redefinition of previously familiar terms: *connection* no longer necessarily follows *human;* and *social* implies not togetherness and community, but silence and isolation.

You never have to be alone in iPhone World. If you'll just renounce this last stubborn vestige of the old life, this antiquated (and frankly vain) insistence on the privilege of being meaningfully alone with your thoughts and feelings, then you never again have to be *alone* at all.

This is the implicit promise, and it presents not with a shriek of metal, a cloud of smoke, and the whistle's shrill call in the virgin forest, but in a glowing and reverent silence—a silence far deeper than that which hung over Walden Pond, and one born of an isolation so total and seamless that, had old Henry been around to pay witness, he just may have had to rethink the wisdom of keeping quite so sober.

~

Five years after I'd moved on from Casa de Agave and shortly after leaving New Mexico with my freshly minted MFA, I briefly found myself at loose ends and working there again. Tending bar obviously wasn't the most ambitious of career paths, especially not after a combined six years of graduate school, but I needed a job that provided a decent income while still allowing me time to write. That, and I suppose I felt something like a modern version of the lament near the end of *Walden* where Thoreau says he'd prefer "not to live in this restless, nervous, bustling, trivial Nineteenth Century, but stand or sit thoughtfully while it goes by."

A bar seemed as good a place to stand as any, and it was nice to see the old crew—Jim and Juan Antonio were still easy to work for, Arturo and Bentley were still regulars, and Caesar had been promoted to manager—but something felt different. The place was largely unchanged, the décor still tasteful and the walls still mercifully devoid of televisions. Happy hour featured the same cheap cerveza and half-price margaritas, and the Baja lobster remained fresh and good.

So, was the change I sensed actually a change in myself? Maybe, although in comparison to the culture at large, I was sunk to my knees in mud. Because that intimate horseshoe bar was no longer particularly festive. What had once seemed a world apart, a little enclave remote from the pressures of workaday reality, now felt more like everywhere else. Where it'd once been pleasantly raucous, it was now sedate, glowing and anxiously quiet. Now, instead of hustling to serve the lively crowd their desired social lubricants, I wordlessly mixed drinks for strangers lost in the depths of social media.

A few years later, I would walk into that airport bar in Texas and see the logical conclusion of all this, but during my second go-round at Casa de Agave, I was still resisting the inevitable. Or maybe I was just in denial that the romanticized feelings I'd long harbored for bars and bartending really were dying a high-speed, 4G, e-death.

"Arturo," I said, unnerved by the ring of ghostly faces, "look at everybody . . ."

He glanced up from his own phone and smirked. "We don't live in the real world anymore, dude. This is iPhone World."

I looked across the room at Caesar, who now spent his nights at the host stand, staring in thinly veiled Sartrean anguish at the device hidden in his lap. In fact, Caesar reminded me of a character from Edward Hopper—although without that sense of peace in his loneliness. I might've turned to Bentley in hopes of getting a more upbeat take on things, but he'd been coming in less frequently of late, having taken to meeting dates not in the bar, but on Grindr.

I spoke quietly to Arturo. "I don't think I want to live in iPhone World."

"Nobody does." His eyes flicked away from his screen and then back again. "That's why we're all here."

A line that might've come straight from *No Exit*. A moment later, I asked the logical follow up. "But if everyone just wants to drink alone, why bother coming to a bar?"

"We all drink alone in iPhone World," Arturo said. "That's the whole point."

With that, I mixed him another cocktail unasked.

As for myself, I was still hanging on to my old flip-phone, but I understood it was just a matter of time before I'd have to join the crowd. Call me a fatalist, but Thoreau (and Caesar) were right: for better or worse and regardless of the price, the future is a smoke-belching locomotive steaming down tracks already laid. And while Thoreau warned that men tend to become the tools of their tools, and that people believe they ride upon the railroad when the reality is just the opposite, if Henry were writing today, *Walden* would be self-published on Amazon and available for Kindle download at $1.99.

Such is the world, though, and perhaps it's best not to dwell. Then again, consider an event from a few weeks later.

One of the new batch of regulars—a lanky twentysomething named Ben—stumbled into Casa de Agave with a badly bloodied nose. His shirt was ruined, and his fingers looked to have been dipped in red paint. Alarmed, I came around the bar with a clean towel and took him by his bony shoulder and steered him down onto a stool. He blubbered and stammered for a while, but I kept talking to him and patting him on the back and asking what in the world had happened, how he'd come by his injury, whether he was okay, and if I should call for help.

Towel pressed to his face and openly weeping from shock, Ben finally managed to explain that he'd been mugged. He'd been on his way to the bar, crossing the avenue just a block down while FaceTiming a friend to meet up, when out of nowhere a guy sucker punched him. He hadn't even seen his attacker—hadn't even noticed him coming.

Then I understood. "This guy stole your phone?"

Ben nodded, his blood and tears pinking that clean white towel.

While he was inconsolable that night, not forty-eight hours later I saw Ben again. A fat nose and two black eyes notwithstanding, he seemed his usual carefree self.

I asked if the police had caught the man who attacked him.

"Oh gosh, listen to this," he said. "So, just a couple weeks ago I downloaded this totally amazing app that tracks your phone's whereabouts in real time . . ."

Sure enough, the app had helped the police locate his assailant. Then Ben pulled the recovered device from his pocket and held it up between us such that I could no longer quite see the features of his bruised and battered face. As he began to caress the screen with the tips of his pale fingers, a flickering glow lit his forehead and the edge of his jaw.

A moment later, his polite but oddly faraway voice asked me—or perhaps someone like me, some fellow passenger of a certain utility—for a margarita on the rocks.

10

DRAMMING WITH FRANK O'BRIEN

As this narrative attests, I've worked with a lot of colorful characters over the years—bars attract oddballs of all stripes—but much of what made those people unique is lost to me now. Lost, that is, in a haze of late nights, too many drinks, and whatever largely inconsequential crap I happened to be preoccupied with back then.

There are a select handful of people, though, the ones in this book, whom I still recall vividly. And as a guy who writes it seems incumbent upon me to try and express who they were when I knew them, to paint a sort of portrait . . .

≈

Although he prided himself a man's man, a busted-knuckle brawler and midnight cocksman of near-mythic status, he had a soft spot for Italian loafers. In fact, anytime the brown leather toeboxes got splashed with sour mix or triple sec, he'd stop mid-service, wet a cocktail napkin with soda water from the gun, and dab those shoes of his clean.

He was also the one who taught me about Halfers—whereby a beer is split and clandestinely chugged on the clock—along with the finer points of Service Chicken—a contest of wits and wills whereby bartenders compete to see who can avoid serving annoying customers for the longest amount of time—and while I couldn't keep up when it came to Halfers and though I never once prevailed in Service Chicken (he would feign distraction, deafness, dementia; whatever it took) the point lay in continuity of ritual.

Because ritual was important to him. He'd been behind the stick at Casa de Agave on Friday and Saturday nights for years before we began working together—from the time I left for Jenny Lake until I came back after finishing my degree in New Mexico—and he'd secured the money shifts through a combination of charm, speed under pressure, and sufficient cunning to see fired those not to his liking. And despite an initial skepticism of me ("I had you pegged for a narc," was how he put it), over the months a rough trust bloomed between us and he saw fit to pass down his knowledge of Dramming—an antiquated Scots-Irish term connoting the tradition whereby distillery hands tasted product throughout the workday as a nod to both quality control and morale.

Consider first the Casual Lefty, which turns upon resisting the rookie urge to sneak-pour under the rail, that deadest of dead giveaways. Instead, like a magician who dupes by misdirection, glassware is lined up in plain sight and cocktails banged out with the busy right hand—scooping ice, pouring booze, mixing juices, sprinkling bitters—whereas the forgotten left hand remains busier still. Or the Long Count, the gist of which is to pour not into the mixing glass but rather the shaker tin itself, a reversal to conceal the volume dispensed and thereby turn four-counts into eights and eights into sixteens and sixteens into total oblivion. Finally, the No Choicer, that ballsiest of moves wherein one drinks right alongside the regulars. Should management or ownership take umbrage, the regs demanded it, and—assuming said regs have been sufficiently greased—they'll swear on their mothers' honor that the only reason they just dropped sixty bucks on a round was for the joy of doing a shot with their favorite bartender.

Beyond even these venerable techniques, in time he saw fit to share his most sacred of bar wisdoms. And though we disagreed politically ("Any man who votes Democrat either keeps a cat for a pet or wears pink panties under his Levis," he said, knowing full well I both supported President Obama and had a litterbox in my apartment), and while his take on romantic love was determinist at best ("When it comes to women, just remember what Darwin said: Only Dicks Get Pussy"), and despite the questionable ethics of his long-term financial strategy ("Unless you wanna die behind the oak with a blown-out liver, you gotta train the regs to Play Ball," he'd often say, with Playing Ball being a tacit agreement whereby barflies are egregiously undercharged on the understanding they'll wildly over-tip: a fifty-dollar tab becomes twenty, and what would've been a ten-dollar gratuity suddenly doubles, resulting in twenty made and twenty saved for all involved)—no, as different as we were in outlook and temperament, I cannot now say I didn't learn from him, or even that these silly-seeming things won't linger in my memory and perhaps even bequeath one last bitter chuckle on my deathbed.

So, a grifter, yes, but a charismatic one. An Irish-Catholic boy from the Windy City who'd somehow gotten lost on his way home from Murphy's one night only to wash up on the beach in San Diego where the people were soft and life was easy, but where the deep-dish pie couldn't sniff Lou Malnati's jockstrap. Get a couple of Heinekens in him and he'd quote Mike Ditka, a few more and he'd reminisce on the days when breakfast meant hot dogs and brews in the bleacher seats at Wrigley. His shaven head was knotted with scars from years working the club scene ("You hop over the rack feet first, grab the douchebag by the collar of his shiny fucking shirt, and then just wail away like the hockey players do").

Truthfully, though, his wilder days were in the rearview by then. He was still beefy through the shoulders, but well on his way to fat ("The old lady made me give up the smokes") as well as happily married—to a former coworker, no less, that selfsame old lady whom he'd wooed by requesting she do him the honor of tucking in his shirttail each night before he got behind the stick ("A creepy move, sure, but that's how I knew she was into me").

When the time finally came for me to make a move of my own, and I put in my two weeks' notice at Casa de Agave yet again, he took the news surprisingly hard—"Of all the rejects and jerkoffs and dipshits I've bartended with over the years," he said, "you were the best of 'em"—and not a month later, I heard through a mutual friend that he'd done one too many Halfers and gotten fired after a round of Service Chicken reached its logical conclusion. While I suspect that last move may not have been entirely accidental, and although he's since retired from the bar game for good and become the proud father of two rowdy boys and one lovely daughter, I'll always remember him the way he was behind the oak: quick with a one-liner, terrific with people, happy to play the asshole, and tenderhearted on the sly.

He was Frank O'Brien, a barman's barman if ever there was one.

11

ISLAND FEVER

Talk around the island was that a strain of flesh-eating bacteria had taken a local's arm.

He'd been out for a swim, apparently. Maybe he'd had a cut or scrape that he neglected to bandage, or perhaps his skin was merely abraded—sunburned even. Whatever the case, that delicate shell that kept him separate from the universe was breached, and in short order he found himself an amputee. No one seemed to know exactly where the man had been swimming. It might've been anyplace. Blue water was all around: the sea, the bay, the coves, even the misting rain that drifted over the island each afternoon, wicked from the air by the Norfolk pines planted in Dole Park and along the footpath leading up to Koele.

None of my coworkers seemed particularly troubled by the news, though. Yes, it was awful for the man involved—scary, weird, horrible—but it was nothing for the rest of us to worry or brood over. Nothing, that is, to feel melancholy about.

≈

As my thirties crept toward their precipitous middle, I found myself at even looser ends. I was now the not-quite-proud possessor of a Juris Doctorate *and* a Master's in Fine Arts, but I still hadn't published a book, and you can't land a somewhat-decent teaching job without a book (or three), with somewhat-decent teaching jobs being the de facto compensation offered up to writers in a country that no longer compensates its writers. So, instead of publishing and career progress, I was working at Casa de Agave again while trying (and failing) to relive a more-or-less happy stretch of my long-lost twenties.

And then there was that day when I sat reading and Bart crawled onto my lap. While we'd been friends and allies for years, he'd never really shard my taste for literature, so I brushed his tail aside and tried to concentrate. But he was particularly persistent, purring and head-butting the pages and studying me with his quizzical green eyes. So, I laid the book aside and petted him, only to feel the ridges of his spine. When had he gotten so thin? His jaunty little potbelly was mostly gone, too. I'd noticed he'd lost a few pounds but wrote it off to a switch in brands of kibble. He'd done no vomiting or complaining, and he still spent his days in his accustomed manner, lounging outside the apartment and keeping our stoop free of trespassing doves and pigeons.

Feeling around his neck, suddenly concerned, I discovered a pea-sized nodule hiding beneath the felt of his collar. He didn't flinch when I touched it. Not tender, apparently. A swollen lymph node, or maybe an abscess from scrapping with the dirty neighbor cats?

A week later, the nodule was a marble. The veterinarian shined a light in his mouth. "Look," she said. Far down his throat, barely visible, hid an angry red egg. I asked about surgery, but the vet shook her head and explained how cats are susceptible to cancer because they clean themselves with their mouths. "The world's full of poison," she said. "In the grass, the rain. And this mass is aggressive. Even if he survived the operation, it'd just grow right back."

I took him home, another appointment already made. After calling in sick to work, I held a living wake. The tumor, seemingly emboldened by discovery, now grew so fast that Bart could no longer swallow solid food. So, I bought a carton of half-and-half that he could comfortably lap from a dish. For me, a bottle of Evan Williams sour mash. As the level in that bottle sank, so did the milk in the carton. On the appointed day, I followed the vet into an area off the exam room and scratched my old friend behind the ears as she ran a needle into his leg.

Just a few days later, I was working up the resolve to finally toss out his leftover flea meds and cat food, when my phone rang. "It's Grandma," my mother said.

My maternal grandmother was in her late nineties by then, so no surprises, but still I had no words. My mother had cared for Grandma through those last bad years. Through a broken hip and surgery, through incontinence and night terrors and into the depths of dementia and blackest depression. My mother listened quietly as her own mother stated time and again that she wanted to die. That this was no way to live. That her life was over—although it wasn't, not quite. All of this my mother had born more or less alone, with a stoicism I can hardly fathom.

I purchased a suit—the first I'd owned since law school—and flew back to Illinois. At the funeral, I sat beside my mother in a chapel in the small town where Grandma had lived, listening to a preacher tell unconvincing stories about her life. Hairless and pale, he bore an uncanny resemblance to Billy Corgan of The Smashing Pumpkins. Try as I might, I couldn't stop those old songs from running through my head as that odd-looking man promised salvation via the Gospels of Matthew, pretending all the while to have known a woman whose name—even then, even as he spoke over her open casket—sounded so unsure on his lips that I feared he'd bungle it.

Had I been the one speaking that day, I'd have told the story of how throughout my boyhood Grandma steadfastly refused to accompany my mother and me to Pizza Hut on our trips to visit. Although it was the only pizza place in town, Grandma was peculiarly obstinate on this point. It was as if the franchise had personally offended her somehow. When, on one such visit, my mother finally demanded to know why and what the big deal was, Grandma balled her small fists on her hips, narrowed her pale blue eyes and declared, "Because Pizza Hut is a *saloon!*"

Sure enough, the pizzeria served beer, which made it every bit as disreputable as some Dodge City bordello full of gambling and pistol smoke. Remembering this, I took a last look at my grandmother. Makeup covered a bruise above her right eye. Evidence of a fall, of disequilibrium, of the ordinary horrors of time and gravity. I tried to remember her when she'd been younger, doddering about the tiny kitchen that her husband—a grandfather who died before I got the chance to meet him—built with his own Irish hands. How she loved that kitchen, that cozy house. How much pride she'd taken in her modest home.

Once back in California, though, alone in that spartan apartment, my own lack of any real home seemed clearer than ever. And so, tether-less, career-less, plan-less, and even cat-less, I decided to hit the road yet again. But this time the road was considerably longer and entailed a one-way ticket to Oceania—more specifically, to the island of Lana'i, Hawai'i.

～

Lana'i is known as "the private isle." Once controlled by the Mormons and then by Maunalei Sugar and later Dole (formerly it was "the pineapple isle"), it's now held by the software mogul Larry Ellison, a man whose preposterous yacht could often be seen at anchor in Hulopo'e Bay. This just past a crescent of pristine beach that constituted the backdrop of my latest bartending gig. The sushi empire Nobu had opened an outlet in the Four Seasons resort, and the pay and benefits were unusually good, as Lanaians had unionized for equitable salaries and health insurance, vacation time and sick days. The job was something of an afterthought, though, as foremost was my desire to escape a mainland life on the slow boat to nowhere. And where better than Hawai'i for that? My landlocked imagination foresaw a shimmering turquoise idyll. Waves breaking on golden sand. Volcanoes and rum-runner sunsets. Rolling into work at dusk, cologned in saltwater and suntan oil after a day spent basking in the tropical sun.

Naïve as all that now sounds, Oceania's clichés are powerful: surfing and hula, campfires on the beach and pig roasts, and women with nut-brown suntans and lilikoi blossoms in their hair. Such images have driven men not unlike myself into the salt desert of the Pacific for centuries, and I suppose I felt something like the call of the exotic. That, and Lana'i constituted yet another chance to shed my accustomed skin—to move, to start afresh.

I'd had a number of fresh starts before, however. And hadn't those other moves, though less ambitious geographically, been born of much the same desire? Wherever you go, there you are, of course, and I couldn't reasonably expect to take anyone besides myself with me to Lana'i. By this point, I'd traveled enough to understand all that, even if some stubborn part of me hoped it were otherwise. Looking back, the move to the islands wasn't really a rational decision. Instead, I felt compelled, drawn in my unmooring, as if some dark thing were rising in my system that only still more *going* could ease.

Perhaps the pull of exoticism is not unlike certain strains of malaria: a sickness that lingers dormant in the liver only to reenter the bloodstream again and again?

On the Fourth of July, our restaurant staff gathered at the remnants of Club Lana'i on Polihua Beach, to barbecue and compete in the first annual Nobu Olympics. There would be a tug-of-war and an egg-toss and other events, all culminating in a potato sack race—a bit of drama to cap off the day's festivities.

Originally, Club Lana'i had been a party spot for Maui tourists, but now lay abandoned. Secluded on the windward north shore, it was easier reached by boat than by my tumbledown Jeep (an "island cruiser" with roach traps under the seats and bungee cords holding the doors shut), and the vibes were surreal. Ramshackle huts stood partially collapsed, staves missing here and there, thatch roofs shot through with light, all of it melting board by board back into the forest. Sticks of sun-bleached bamboo furniture lay scattered about and what had once been a koi pond had devolved into a rank green puddle. The vacant and sunlit grounds gave the sense that someone might soon return—not tourists, but the *huaka'i po*, or Night Marchers, those ghostly warriors of island lore, pounding drums and garbed in tattered helmets and cloaks.

After saying howzit to my coworkers and talking a little story (and contributing the requisite beer and shrimp for the barbecue), I wandered away from the volleyball and music and looked across the Kalohi Channel at the neighboring island of Moloka'i and Kamakou, the highest point of an extinct volcano chain, its jade peak capped in misty clouds.

While Moloka'i is known as "the friendly isle," its history tells a different story. In the nineteenth century, victims of Hansen's disease were sequestered on the remote Kalaupapa Peninsula. With the Hawaiian population lacking natural immunity, total and lifelong isolation was believed the only option. From 1866 onward, over 8,000 people, most of them native Hawaiians, were banished to the colony. Eventually, a priest from Belgium, Father Damien de Veuster, came to tend (and convert) the sick, and he organized the leprosarium that still stands today, now a historic site home to a last few elderly lepers.

Exactly one century and five years before that day on Polihua Beach, on the Fourth of July 1908, Jack London visited Kalaupapa. As with the Nobu Olympics, the colony's residents spent the holiday engaged in sport. First, a horse race in which a Portuguese boy bested a Chinese boy by a nose. Watching this, London found himself carried away with excitement, cheering and tossing his hat right alongside the lepers. Next was a donkey race, but with a catch—the contestants rode mounts provided by one another—and thus the lepers entered only their most obstreperous of animals. London describes these races in comic terms, with donkeys wandering off the track under their befuddled riders, all to the delight of the joyous lepers. At the end of the day, London even passed out awards for best costume and horsemanship.

His aim in writing like this was to help dispel some of the fear surrounding the disfiguring disease, one that had carried a stigma of biblical sin since its first appearance during the Crusades. He goes on, however, to describe leprosy's penchant for lying dormant, how the infection will flare and ravage a patient, only to recede and wait for years or even decades. Might this bear comparison to the exotic itself—a thing that once it's gotten hold of you lives inside your flesh, quietly waiting to flare?

Then a present-day vision that London surely would've appreciated: one of the local guys, a hotel porter, had scaled a leaning palm. Hand over hand he went, higher and higher, his bare feet miraculously adherent two stories above the deer-tracked sand. Everyone had paused to watch his daring climb. Once atop the tree, this lithe character hacked loose a coconut and let it drop. A moment later, one of my coworkers unfolded a pocket knife, cored the nut, and filled it from a bottle of Buffalo Trace. "We call this a Kentucky coconut," he said, and passed it to me.

And so I turned away from the green pyramid of Kamakou and drank in the sight of my friends, the beer on ice, the fish browning on the grill, the sunshine and water and light. Someone cranked the music and a breeze wafted across the channel from Maui way, and just then a trio of waitresses ran down the long splintery dock, laughing and jiggling in their bikinis, before leaping hand-in-hand into the sea. But vivid as it all was, the present felt slippery, and my thoughts drifted away only to settle upon another haole come to Lana'i in search of the exotic, one who, as with Jack London, had sympathized with those diseased people abandoned across the channel.

～

In the early 1860s, a missionary with the Church of Latter-day Saints named Walter Murray Gibson came to the island. Gibson's grand scheme (proposed to Brigham Young by Gibson himself) involved developing ranchland and proselytizing the natives. Lana'i would be a new City of Joseph, a place the ever-persecuted Mormons might call home.

Gibson had converted at thirty-eight, however, which is a little late in the game for religious epiphany, and his background was suspect at best. As a younger man, he'd purchased a boat (the *Flirt*), and hatched a scheme to run guns to the fledgling dictatorship in Guatemala. After failing as an arms smuggler, he sailed to colonial Java, where he was arrested by the Dutch on suspicion of planning to incite a coup. A year and a half later, he escaped in daring fashion, dodging cannon fire and narrowly avoiding having his neck stretched from a yardarm—that, or the Dutch simply let him go. Much of Gibson's life is this way: of dual accounts.

Consider his return from Java, upon which he met Nathaniel Hawthorne (who was working as a consul in England) and spun a tale so tall and gothicky that Hawthorne himself might've written it, the upshot being that he, Gibson, had been switched at birth and denied the privileges of his noble bloodline. Later, he also apparently forged a letter of recommendation from President Franklin Pierce.

Unsurprisingly, Gibson was also a talented writer; he authored well-received books on his time with the Dutch (*The Prisoner of Weltevreden*) and on personal wellness (*Sanitary Instructions for Hawaiians*), and later founded a pro-Hawaiian newspaper on Oahu that was a thorn in the heel of the powerful haole landowners who aspired to dominate the kingdom. Largely due to this advocacy, in 1882 Gibson was appointed Prime Minister by King Kalakaua.

Shortly after coming to Lana'i, however, Gibson was excommunicated from the Mormon Church on reports that the self-proclaimed "High Priest of Melchizedek" was plotting to militarize the young men and invade other islands. Additionally, it was said he'd trained the Hawaiians to view him as a god, à la Colonel Kurtz. Gibson insisted these accusations were slander, but the church nonetheless determined he'd undermined Brigham Young's authority. Most damning of all, the excommunication documents reveal that Gibson had "introduced pagan superstitions, and encouraged such vicious practices as hula dancing."

Thus, Gibson transitioned from proselytizer to gentleman rancher. But restlessness still hounded him. Since youth, he'd been inexplicably infected with the idea that Oceania was where he'd finally make his mark, the place where his life would become truly extraordinary. In the years to follow, however, his focus shifted from capital accumulation to the winning of political capital. As such, he threw himself more fully into his Oahu newspaper venture, where he often used his soapbox to advocate for the victims of leprosy.

Native Hawaiians who contracted the disease were denounced by the white ruling class as *ma'i pāke*, or unclean—an allusion to syphilis, which had devastated the islanders after its introduction in the time of Cook—but Gibson didn't abide this racism. In fact, it was Gibson who recruited a group of Catholic nuns to nurse the afflicted (he fell hopelessly in love with one of them, of course), and ultimately published the pleas that brought Father Damien to Kalaupapa.

By the end of his days, flesh whittled away by consumption and his political enemies brandishing knives, Gibson was fully invested in the fight to protect indigenous Hawaiians, and the care of lepers was one highly visible and emotional aspect of that cause. He'd begun life dreaming of the exotic as a route to wealth and power, but something changed him. Maybe it was the plight of the lepers, or maybe it was the islands themselves, the beauty of the land and the fragility of the culture. In this way, we can see the life of Walter Murray Gibson as not merely that of a charismatic opportunist, but a man whose pursuit of the exotic transformed over time into nothing less than a realization of his own better self.

≈

My partner in the Nobu Olympics was a heavyset yet reliably lighthearted waiter named Javier, who wore an elaborate pompadour and waxed the tips of his piratical mustache. Having noticed that I lifted weights at the island gym each morning, Javier had recruited me with visions of a sweep, of our taking first place and leaving Club Lana'i with the nifty little engraved trophy our restaurant manager had special ordered through Amazon.

But I was having trouble concentrating on the day's events, and all that weightlifting wasn't done for the sake of athleticism. Nor was it out of concern for my health, or even simple vanity. No, the brutal workouts were the only thing that eased my chronic anxiety and relieved, if only for an hour or two, the darkness of my thought patterns. I relished the absurd agony of pressing hundred-pound cast-iron dumbbells, and I needed the nervous shock of deadlifting sums so heavy that the gym's rusty barbells bowed like toothpicks. Never mind that I was old enough to know better than to push my body so hard. Never mind the three knee reconstructions, the shredded cartilage and crepitus and pain. Let alone that hernia in my abdomen, or my chronically impinged shoulder. No, all such injuries paled in comparison to the unquiet inside my own skull.

The joys of the writing life weren't exactly helping, either. I'd come to the island with a number of manuscripts moldering in limbo—the two irredeemable novels I'd already taken out behind the barn and shot, but now yet another novel, rough but better, this time a dark comedy about hapless car salesmen in rural Illinois; there was also a series of literary essays, most having to do with my life in bars—and to abandon these new projects, unpromising as they may have seemed, was unthinkable. But the experience of picking over their bones, of trying to breathe life into their stitched-together corpses, was not unlike the helplessness of unrequited love. While I was wise enough by then to harbor no illusions as to undiscovered genius, I'd given a lot to writing, and all seemingly in vain. Investments of time, most obviously, but also opportunities forsaken and a concurrent lack of stability in all ways conventionally relevant: financial, personal, emotional. Often, it felt like I'd flushed the better part of my youth down the toilet.

And so perhaps I'd thought Oceania would help clarify my writing, or that life on a private island would discipline my habits, or even that whatever my words lacked would be miraculously found on that little red rock in the middle of the sea, an illusion not unlike that which drove Walter Murray Gibson. Whatever the case, it turned out I was the same writer on Lana'i as back on the mainland, only now I also suffered a suspicion that real life (and thus the stuff of real art) was happening thousands of miles away, in the very cities I'd abandoned.

My instincts weren't entirely off-base, though. Art and the exotic have a connection, and one not restricted to writers such as London or Stevenson or

Twain, who famously traveled there. In fact, it's possible our finest depiction comes courtesy of Somerset Maugham's *The Moon and Sixpence,* which is loosely based on the life of Paul Gauguin. At the heart of this slim novel is Charles Strickland, an English stockbroker who inexplicably throws away career and stability at age forty, declaring that he intends to paint, that he *must* paint, and that he has no more feelings to spare for his wife ("Love is a disease") or his children ("They've had a good many years of comfort..."), and all of this despite his having little training in the arts. Undeterred, Strickland travels first to Paris— where he starves, paints, and eventually seduces and drives to suicide the wife of a sympathetic fellow painter—before, like his model Gauguin, he vanishes into Polynesia.

The book's narrator is a young and moderately successful writer, but one distinctly aware of his own lack of genius. By way of contrast, he describes Strickland's art as the work of a man possessed, a sensualist in a dream world of his own creation. This tension sets up the story's end, which finds Strickland living in the primitive jungle, "unmindful of the world and by the world forgotten." A doctor is sent for by Strickland's native wife (a marriage of convenience) and the doctor is horrified to see that Strickland has contracted leprosy. Upon his death, Strickland's masterpiece is discovered, a primeval vision of mankind's origins, images "beautiful and obscene," and all painted on the walls of the hut in which he'd suffered and died. As a final outrageous touch, the shaken doctor notes that leprosy had blinded Strickland, thereby driving home the conceit of artistic genius being more infection and curse than gift.

All of this might be just colorful melodrama, but for a passage that riffs on dislocation and the happenstances of birth. "I have an idea," Maugham writes, "that some men are born out of their due place . . . Perhaps it is this sense of strangeness that sends men far and wide in search of something permanent, to which they may attach themselves." That something permanent, it seems, that necessary object of attachment, has to do not with exotic landscapes or people, but with some hard-to-descry vision of the self. For Maugham's fictionalized Gauguin, it was the mystery of disappearing into art, whereas for Walter Murray Gibson it was the need for a place where he might recast his soul. Both of these examples illuminate the call of the exotic in certain ways, but like malaria and consumption and leprosy, island fever has many strains.

～

While the ruins of Club Lana'i bore a passing resemblance to the Tahitian setting of Strickland's mysterious death, in one of our beer-fueled breaks between events, perhaps owing to the sight of Moloka'i and echoes of leprosy, I found myself thinking not of Strickland but once again of that unfortunate local who'd bumped into the flesh-eating bacteria. What bum luck: to go for a swim in your home waters, only for some insidious and invisible thing to steal away a limb. Moreover, the sight of the other islands and the channels between reminded me of the relationship between myself and my fellow Lanaians, both native and haole. Gulfs, choppy and blue, and ones I hadn't the compass to navigate.

But I was alone in such gloomy thinking; everyone else was having fun. Javier and I had actually made a decent showing, as well. We'd dominated the tug-of-war, held our own in the egg-toss, and placed second or third in an event that involved the seriocomic hands-free transfer of toilet paper rolls from broomsticks clutched between teammates' legs. There were other events I can't now recall (blame the Kentucky Coconut), but I do remember feeling ill at ease and distracted—a symptom of my inveterate melancholia (to borrow a phrase from Robert Burton, the Renaissance-era author of *The Anatomy of Melancholy*), a condition that the islands had done little to abate. This is the nature of inveteracy, though, and by age thirty-three I'd come to suspect that no relief was to be found. Not through pills, not through talk, and certainly not through writing. The black dog was just a part of me, inseparable, and while the condition was not disfiguring like leprosy or whatever bug had mutilated that local man, it was stigmatizing and isolating in its way.

Melancholia (so much more graceful a term than *depression,* that banal misnomer) was something I'd learned not to speak of. No one wants to hear about the inexplicable sadness of young and basically healthy people—especially those who make a handsome living pouring cocktails on a Hawaiian island—and that's understandable. But melancholia is misunderstood. It isn't really sadness. Elements of that, sure, but it's not ultimately an emotion. Instead, it's a lens, a darkling glass, an affliction and a potentially fatal disorder—but also, I suspect, a symbiosis that can sometimes act as a strange gift. As the aging Walter Murray Gibson suggests, having gone from religious chicanery and dreams of Pacific empire to recruiting nuns and priests to tend the victims of leprosy, our capacity for empathy reflects our ability to accept and endure sustained disappointment, much as humility often turns upon an awareness of mortality.

That said, I'd come to Lana'i in the subconscious hope of reprieve. Exhausted with myself, I'd felt a fever building. I had to escape, or at least find some distraction, and the islands called. Their exoticism had seemed, amid the hordes and gridlock of California, like a last resort, a rolling blue that might pacify that part of myself I was simultaneously most fascinated by and most wary of: the part that allowed me to write authentically, but could also leave me essentially wordless, sometimes for months at a stretch.

A private island? You bet, in all the ways we might imagine one: remote and inaccessible, skeptical of modernity and hostile to it demands, and marked by that weird secular mysticism that aims to hold the world and time at bay. This sort of exoticism—this purposeful marooning of the self—is not unlike a latent sickness. As with melancholy, it's difficult to say whether the etiology stems from within or without. Is it the allure of tropical waters and the warmth of a Polynesian sun, or some invisible but keenly felt glitch? Moreover (and again like melancholy), this fever can be seductively pleasant at first; you want to revel in it, to explore its murky corners and let it lull you away from the ordinary. Only later does it turn and show its true face, its lion-face, but by then it's already settled in the veins.

This world of ours often lacks a sense of the necessary gravitas, though, and soon enough it was time for the potato sack race.

≈

Soft afternoon light slanted down upon Javier as he toed the starting line, sheathed to the waist in a burlap bag. Our coworkers had formed a tunnel along the track, everyone jeering and razzing. I thought again of Jack London watching the lepers of Moloka'i celebrate Independence Day, misrepresenting, if for charitable reasons, an hour's reprieve as true happiness.

Then Nobu's general manager, playing London's role as official master of ceremonies, raised a cap gun starter pistol. "Ready! . . . On your marks! . . . Get set! . . ."

Pop!

Burlap bag clutched to his waist, Javier galloped off. Twenty yards down, he pirouetted as gracefully as an intoxicated 265-pound waiter can possibly pirouette and hurtled back toward me. Oily pompadour pasted to his brow, waxed mustache tips abuzz like humming bird wings, he burst across the line trailing a cloud of sand and dust.

He'd managed to give us a lead on our closest competitors, a husband-and-wife team from the kitchen. But now it was my turn, and upon climbing into the bag I realized it wasn't big enough. My size-15 feet filled the entire bottom, and the sack was too short for my considerable height—the hem barely reached my thighs—the upshot being that, instead of shuffling along like everyone else, I had to bend and jump to produce forward momentum. Beside me, the diminutive Japanese cook-wife zoomed away, dainty feet wiggling under the burlap.

"Put your beer down and go!" Javier shouted.

So, I kangarooed forth and actually moved pretty well, so well that I made up ground on the cook-wife. At track's end, I turned on a half-dollar and dug deep for the homestretch. Mere yards left, the crowd roaring, I bent low for what would've been a tremendous and ultimately race-winning broad jump—except I struck a patch of sand that wasn't sand, but rock.

Stumbling, the potato sack coiled around my ankles, and I heard something odd: another *pop!*

I landed hard and rolled. Grit peppered my flesh and groans rose from the boozy peanut gallery. The cook-wife was long gone. One potato sack after another hustled past me and across the finish line. Javier chucked his beer in disgust.

Race lost, I extricated myself from the burlap and limped off the course. I was filthy from rolling on the ground while coated in sweat and sunblock, and was about to take a dip in the sea to wash off, but then I considered what invisible threats might lurk in the water. So, instead, I rested in the shade of a palm as the festivities carried on behind me, without me.

Like Jack London back on the Fourth of July 1908, I've done my best here to describe these races and games in comic terms, but—as was the sober reality of London's visit to Kalaupapa—it wasn't really all that funny, or at least not for me. Because as I sat there studying the silent bulk of Kamakou and nursing the last sweet milk from a Kentucky coconut, my ballooning right foot turned the same deep and lovely blue as the afternoon swells.

≈

It took months for the fracture to heal, and I spent most of that time back on the mainland. First, I'd planned to stay with a brother in rural Indiana, but being possessed of a keen sense of timing, he decided to file for divorce a week after my arrival. Thus, I bought a used vehicle (from a pair of local nuns, no less) and hit the road.

In a bar in Omaha, a young woman smiled at me. She was doing an internship in architecture. She was lonely. A month later, seeming less lonely—and also perhaps tired of the sight of me run aground on her couch with a laptop and a beer—she asked me to move out.

After that, I drove to New Mexico to visit my old writing professors, and there I happened to meet another young woman in another bar. But, again, we were a cure for each other's loneliness for only so long. Then it was off to Las Vegas, where a cocktail waitress I'd once worked with had some time to spare before her father returned to their shared condo. Then it was down to San Diego, where I crashed with a series of old friends and lovers, spending my mornings working on that unlikely sounding novel about car salesmen and my evenings burning my temporary disability checks in bars.

It may seem this attitude toward love and sex mimicked that of Charles Strickland, but this wasn't really the case. While artistic ambitions do have a way of hamstringing the traditional domestic pose, especially if said artist is temperamentally incapable of staying in one place for any length of time, I was neither cold nor callous. Quite the contrary, I was starved for intimacy and companionship. And yet it was also true that the Stricklandish part of me, the infection of art in an otherwise normal psyche, rendered everything temporary.

Eventually, however, my foot mended. I considered staying on the mainland, settling down somewhere, anywhere, but the Vegas cocktail waitress wasn't returning my calls, and I had no prospects nearly as secure as the job on Lana'i. So, I went back. Almost immediately I knew it for a mistake, though. I slipped back into my routine, working out in the morning, writing in the afternoon, and driving down to the bay to pour drinks come evening—but I suffered from what's commonly referred to as "island fever." Usually, this just means a homesick haole jumps on the nearest plane. I saw it happen to any number of coworkers. Some made it a year, others barely a month. But my particular fever seemed of a different strain, a long-overdue realization about the exotic.

What had seen me to Oceania was, as with Walter Murray Gibson, a desire to kick-start my life into some grander plane, and all mixed up with gullible notions about art, a la Maugham's Charles Strickland. But if it's true that people often feel compelled to explore the terra incognita of their own psyches, it's also true that we blanche in the face of the task's considerable anxiety; and so instead we undertake physical journeys, taxing, expensive, and long, and even though part of us surely suspects that all the miles constitute little but a change of stage dressing for dramas internal. Still, we cling to this emotional escape valve, this fantasy of finding ourselves by putting our bodies somewhere new, even as these restless comings and goings suggest, again and again, that wanderlust is but one way of avoiding a particularly bitter pill: because after finally crawling onto the shore of my own private island, after making that long journey inward and down, it was clear there was nothing particularly unusual or mysterious—nothing, that is, that we might truly call exotic—at bottom of *me*.

There was something there, though. And this thing, this remora, was and is uniquely mine—but it's nothing that requires white sand or palm trees for sustenance. Instead, it's more like a bacteria: something that exists for the most part in a state of dormancy. Something not without interest and a certain potential for empathy, if not even artfulness, but also something isolating and, oftener and oftener it seems, insidious, if only for the vessel acting as its host.

12

COCKTAILS & DREAMS:
ON SKID ROAD WITH LOUIS XIII

"We are Magnificent Digressions, all of us," says the suave but cynical bartender Doug Coughlin in Heywood Gould's *Cocktail*, "We live on the flipside of everyone else's clock . . . Go out into the street and look at the world we've left. Go . . ."

I stumbled upon Gould's dark novel about the nightlife in the spring of 2014, shortly after a job transfer took me from Lana'i to Four Seasons Seattle. But before island fever got the better of me, I chanced to mix a cocktail for none other than Tom Cruise, who plays the young bartender Brian Flanagan—Coughlin's protégé and requisite straight man—in the 1988 film adaptation. Fit as a gymnast and impeccably coiffed, Mr. Cruise seemed to have hardly aged a day in the interim. I half-expected him to start shaking kamikazes and tossing bottles around.

He'd sauntered in fifteen minutes past the night's final seating. At the hostess stand, outfitted in black jeans, black boots, and a lightweight leather coat—as if fresh from the set of *Mission Impossible: Pineapple Island*—he whipped off his designer shades (the sun had set hours before), bathed our beautiful hostess Miliani in one of those famously cocky grins, and requested a prime table.

Later, after his entourage sent back untouched the thirty-two-dollar-an-ounce wagyu steak they'd ordered—an *objet d'art* sizzling medium-rare, asparagus buttery and flaked with rough black pepper, even a quail egg for a touch of *umami* richness—not because there was anything wrong with the cut, but just because, Tom Cruise asked Miliani if she might like to shoot some pool. This was a move he well may have learned from his fictional mentor, the ladies' man Doug Coughlin, with the fallout being that Miliani called in sick the rest of the week, only to see her employment quietly terminated after a few cozy pictures turned up on Instagram.

And that was pretty much it for my brush with Hollywood glamour.

Being the new fish at Four Seasons Seattle, however, I often got stuck working the not-so-glamorous day shifts, juicing citrus and restocking beer and stirring the occasional lunchtime martini while staring idly out the window at the massive Ferris wheel at Pier 57, watching barges tug into Elliott Bay from Asia and commuter ferries cross to Bainbridge Island. Beyond Puget Sound loomed the Olympics, their gloaming peaks tickling the roof of gray clouds, and beyond the mountains lay the Pacific, where I'd spent the last few years getting sunburned and serving saké to vacationers. So, I had plenty of time to mull over my island experience, and after reading Gould's novel and rewatching that old film, both of which feature Brian Flanagan spiriting away to tropical locales to shake luscious mai tais and seduce lonely women, it occurred to me that Tom Cruise had impacted my life more than I may have realized.

And all the while, perched regally on the top shelf behind me, was a figure both Gould and Flanagan would've surely recognized: a bottle of Louis XIII cognac.

~

"Philbert," Abbott said one afternoon, "have you ever seen *Cocktail?*"

This was back in 2006 at the Steelhead, where Abbott and I first met. We'd been discussing my plans, as I'd just put in my two weeks, having decided to slip down I-5 to Southern California and duck the miseries of the coming rainy season following my breakup with Sara.

"That's the one where Tom Cruise flips bottles?"

"Yep, and dances to the Hippy Hippy Shake."

I'd seen the movie years before—or at least bits and pieces, as it was a staple of the late-night cable channels—and I did vaguely recall it. In fact, my first shift behind the bar had gone about as roughly as Tom Cruise's does in the film, both of us having gotten hired on the spot and tossed into the blender with no actual experience. I mentioned this concurrence to Abbott, and he agreed there was a certain similarity between us, a willingness to smile winningly and bullshit our way into jobs, a desperate need for a *Bartender's Bible* to shore up our shaky cocktail recipes, not to mention our glowing repartee with the cocktail waitresses. At the end of the day, though, my being six-foot-six and rather less handsome likely precluded a career switch into acting.

"Wait, doesn't he also get lucky with Elisabeth Shue under a waterfall?"

At this, Abbott fixed me with his pale blue eyes. He was a decade older and had a way of making the frenzied drudgery of restaurant work seem like it'd all somehow be okay, an endearing mix of steady nerves and dark humor. "He goes to the islands," Abbott said, "and snags a gig at a beachfront tourist bar. You know, rum drinks with little tiki umbrellas? He makes a killing."

"Tiki umbrellas? This Irish skin doesn't tan very well."

"Look, all I'm saying is a stint in the islands might be good for you."

I laughed off Abbott's suggestion that day, or so I'd thought. But eight years later, crossing the Pacific at 35,000 feet on a one-way ticket, I recalled his words. Strange to think how an offhand comment like that sinks into the loam of us and seems to vanish, only to rise again and swell and burst in all the roman candle glory of an idea, an adventure, a disaster.

～

While my experience bartending in Oceania was both adventurous and disastrous, after a few months at Four Seasons Seattle, I'd come to see things somewhat differently.

Call it a long-overdue awakening of class-consciousness, or call it veiled envy, or maybe just plain old sadness over the prospect of spending my life doing the bidding of people with money, but the whiskey sours weren't the only thing sour behind the bar. Of course, anyone who works for the Four Seasons realizes they're in the business of pampering wealth, but until you see it up close, until you're knee-deep and can smell it on your hands and taste it on your tongue, it's difficult to fully appreciate the noxious reek of capitalism in these last dying days of empire.

Take the rickety and lipsticked Methuselah who insisted upon toting her forty-ounce Pomeranian (Itsy) to the bar in her oversized and bejeweled Coach purse. Incredibly enough, management ordered me, straight-faced and on multiple occasions, to serve Itsy a lemon drop (sugared rim, of course) in a special two-ounce plastic martini glass kept on hand just for her. After Itsy lapped at and inevitably spilled this drink, her owner would clap and coo with delight—and then chastise me for not sopping up the mess fast enough.

I worked with another bartender named Kolcinski, although he wasn't actually Polish but Latvian, and would glower and mutter curses in his native tongue when inevitably mistaken for Russian. Post-Soviet tensions aside, however, Kolcinski wasn't satisfied with bartending; no, he was studying for his real estate license in hopes of spinning his downtown connections into real loot. The first time Itsy's owner berated me for giving her dog-child a lemon drop to spill, I asked Kolcinski whether everyone around the hotel was really as crazy as they seemed. "You can't beat them," he replied in his graveled voice, "no matter how much you would like to."

Worse than Itsy was Mr. Brooks, an itsy-bitsy and self-described "wealth management consultant" who lived in a multimillion dollar condo upstairs. A financier of the smarmiest sort, Mr. Brooks had attended Washington State University and made a point of proclaiming himself "a Coug" anytime his alma mater showed up on ESPN. He also liked to refer to himself as "alpha male," this born out of a wildly obvious Napoleon complex, one that'd made of him a CrossFit devotee. And with six-pack abs having no purpose except to be seen by other people, Mr. Brooks also had a penchant for appearing shirtless at odd times. He said, "I live upstairs, by the way," to every woman under age forty, and had "accidentally" circulated a series of flatteringly lit dick picks among the gay waitstaff ("It looks pretty big to me," said Damian, a young Peruvian busboy; whereas James, a tall blond server whose athletic wear modeling shots were popular in Japan, said only, "Eh, definitely Photoshopped.").

Most every day, Mr. Brooks would roll into the lounge at happy hour, looking crisp in a tailored suit and five-hundred-dollar shoes. "I'll take an MGD 64," he'd say, "extra cold."

The diet beer was a nod to vanity, whereas the part about "extra cold" was a nod to my position of servility, as if the help couldn't quite be trusted even in such simple matters.

Speaking of cougs and icy temperatures, shortly after Mr. Brooks arrived, Mrs. Brooks would descend from the penthouse. Modelesque, she had five inches on her husband along with a gravity-defying breast-augmentation and a face stapled tight as a snare drum. Rumor was they'd met at the gym, Mrs. Brooks having been elevated from the treadmill of the working class to the cocktail hour ease of the leisure class. She carried vestiges of her background with her, though. At certain moments, you could feel her discomfort with all the hoity-toity foofaraw that came with living at the Four Seasons and being *Mrs. Brooks*. A few years later, long after I was gone, she finally got fed up and left her husband and his various and tawdry infidelities, but back then she was playing her role as best she could.

"Stoli Elite," she would say, never deigning to make eye contact with me. "And don't use regular ice—use a sphere."

These spheres were a racket cooked up by the executive chef and a friend of his who owned a premium ice company. Each morning I'd ride the elevator down to the basement, where amidst a maze of fridges and freezers were these boxes of special ice cubes, each one carefully wrapped in bubbled plastic. Two bucks a sphere? Three? Whatever the case, Seattle had clearly come a long way from its Skid Road days if guys could get rich boxing and selling frozen water.

～

Seattle's Skid Road was the historic track along which logs were oxen-dragged down to the steam mill on Elliott Bay. The old Skid Road effectively divided Seattle in half, with the area to the south known for taverns and missions and brothels, while to the north was the more respectable business and family district. And you can still see remnants of that nineteenth-century divide, as the neighborhoods get rougher the farther one heads south. Today, however, the old Skid Road area around Pioneer Square and Yesler Way (an Ohioan named Henry Yesler owned the mill) is as urban as it gets and no longer remotely working class. In fact, the rapid and steep gentrification of this area (and all the rest of Seattle) has contributed to a glut of homeless people with no hope of affording rent anywhere in the city.

Seven or so blocks north, however—in the heart of downtown and directly across the street from the Four Seasons—is the Hammering Man. A nearly fifty-foot-tall kinetic sculpture made of stainless steel, the big-booted Man stands outside the Seattle Art Museum and slowly swings his hammer twenty hours a day, only resting between one and five in the morning, every day except for Labor Day.

I walked past this slightly misplaced homage to the working class every morning on my way to tend bar, as the route from my apartment to the Four Seasons closely paralleled the historic Skid Road and led right by Pioneer Square. Because now the divide between the haves and have-nots isn't just north-south, but east-to-west, and I lived two-and-a-half miles east, over the steep grades of First Hill in the Central District.

Due to a history of segregationist housing policies, such as redlining and whites-only land sale covenants, the Central District developed as a predominately African-American neighborhood. But it was getting whiter by the minute, as the same Amazon- and Microsoft-driven gentrification that'd made downtown the province of the elite was swiftly flowing east and pushing the old-time residents down into Judkins Park and Columbia City. An ironic reversal of the flow of commerce, as if the Skid Road now ran in reverse—instead of harvested logs sliding down to the mills and sea, money flowed up and over the hills toward the shores of Lake Washington (where Bill Gates lives in a 66,000-square-foot mansion he calls "Xanadu 2.0" in homage to *Citizen Kane*) and high-tech, high-income suburban communities such as Bellevue.

I wasn't really part of the gentrification, though, at least not economically. Growing up, my family had very little money—in rural Illinois, anybody who owned a new pickup and didn't live in a mobile home was considered rich— while as an adult I'd managed to spin a decade of higher education into the previously described unpublishable manuscripts and a career pouring drinks. The basement rooms I rented in the Central District cost less than the price of a single night at the Four Seasons. I heated bean and cheese burritos in a microwave and kept the mini-fridge stocked with whatever beer was on sale at Grocery Outlet.

One morning, shortly after moving in, I'd just begun my long walk to work when an elderly man approached on the sidewalk not half a block from a public swimming pool named after Medgar Evers. I smiled and said good morning, only for the man's eyes to widen as he wobbled past on his cane. "You goddamn white motherfucker," he said.

A month later, walking home around midnight, two young men approached me from the opposite sides of Cherry Street. They stopped just shy of arm's length, having effectively cut me off. The guy on the left, the handsome one, smiled. "Hey, bro," he said, "our car ran out of gas down the street. We need twenty dollars to get home. Can you help us out?"

When I said I had no money, his partner, early twenties, dead-eyed and overweight, asked if I had any silver.

When I said I didn't have any silver either, the first guy turned his head in both directions, scanning the empty street and neighborhood.

"What you got in the backpack?" the second guy said.

Then, just as the handsome one pulled up his shirt to reveal the handgun stuffed in his waistband, I pushed past them and took off running. Whether this was smart or stupid I still can't say, but the foot fracture had healed pretty well by then, and by the hidden gear of speed I found, you'd have thought all those old basketball injuries had never happened at all.

I burst into the scuzzy little bar two blocks down, a place full of Capitol Hill hipsters dressed in skinny jeans and Buddy Holly glasses who thought it gave them street cred to drink their three-dollar PBRs in the general vicinity of black people. Sweaty and shaking badly, I took a stool and kept one eye on the door. But the heavily tattooed bartender must've thought I was either drunk or just plain weird. "Sorry," she said, "but I can't serve you tonight."

Finally, I managed to explain what happened, the attempted mugging, the gun.

"Call an Uber," she said, "if you're too scared to walk."

"Just pour me one whiskey—please?"

"I'm not pouring you jack-shit," she said.

So much for working-class solidarity, I thought.

≈

And as the days and nights wore on at Four Seasons Seattle, I found myself thinking often of social class. I also found myself thinking about *Cocktail*—both versions—and how those stories speak to our supposedly classless society.

In the film, Tom Cruise's Brian Flanagan is young and full of optimism, a fresh-faced kid fresh out of the army and hoping to catch his big break amidst Manhattan's booming bar scene; whereas in Gould's novel, Brian Flanagan is a thirty-eight-year-old burnout who dodged the war in Vietnam by feigning homosexuality ("Don't put me in the barracks with all those guys. I'll go crazy") and who's now facing, as he puts it, "the abyss at the end of Youth." Twenty years behind the oak has left this Brian a borderline suicidal alcoholic with a tenuous grasp on reality. He's a sexist and a womanizer going gray, a drug-abuser and unrepentant thief, a disloyal friend, a bad sibling, and a neglectful son. He's also, no surprise, a writer.

Brian casually references "Gerty Stein," describes his failed novel as alternately "Faulknerian, yet Dreiserian," and he couches that first hellish bar shift, the one with echoes of my own—the botched cocktails, the impatient waitresses, the outraged customers—in terms of Sartre's *No Exit*. His father had been a failed class-warrior, a closet revolutionary, and Brian's childhood home was full of books by Marx and Lenin and other leftist intellectuals. A refugee from the psychedelic generation, Brian has a hard time believing the "Greed is good" ethos of '80s America is anything but a shill and a sham.

Contrast this to Tom Cruise's Brian Flanagan, who boyishly believes in, ardently pursues, and finally gets his very own little slice of the American Dream, in the form of the loving devotion of the aforementioned Ms. Shue, as well as ownership of his own tavern, Cocktails & Dreams, which he plans to franchise and make a fortune.

Things are not so rosy for Gould's Brian Flanagan, though. His love interest, a girl named Mooney, turns out to be a loony—though one with a rich family—and she stalks Brian and finally ropes him into a "solid gold shotgun" marriage. While Brian realizes his new bride is totally nuts, he's happy enough with the tradeoff, as he'll never again have to tend bar.

It's not as if some Hollywood hack came along and gutted Gould's novel, however. No, he's credited with the screenplay as well, though obviously on orders to lighten the mood. I hope he at least got paid handsomely for his troubles. After all, there's a bit early in the novel where Brian Flanagan describes quoting Shakespeare and Robert Service to the screenwriters who frequent his bar, though he doubts whether they can tell the one from the other. Gould himself tended bar in New York in his late thirties, and thus as he mixed cocktails and slid toward "the point of no return," he did so with an up close view—an outsider's view, that of the career proletarian—of all that conspicuous consumption and materialism.

But what interests me most in these parallel stories is their differed take on the American Dream, on money, greed, and the class struggle—ideas that were thrown in my face every single day I stepped behind the oak at Four Seasons Seattle. Because Tom Cruise's *Cocktail* tells the story of an America we'd like to believe in, Horatio Alger's America, the Land of Opportunity, whereas Gould's *Cocktail* tells a story we're hesitant to believe, but one in which we sense some uncomfortable truths. It's the America where poor people mug other poor people at gunpoint, where proletarians scheme and debase themselves for a pittance, where art is a joke unless you can drink it or eat it, and where the abyss at the end of youth is a gallon jug of vodka and a pensioner's garret along Skid Road.

≈

Fitzgerald had it right, though—the rich really do live differently from you and me.

The bar was full of businessmen-types who'd happily give the famous "hundred-dollar-handshake" and slip their bartender a crisp Franklin, if only he could manage to recall their drink from the last time they'd jetted into town. Always a healthy dose of shame in accepting such vainglorious charity but accept it we bartenders would.

Come the weekend, the lounge brimmed over with Armani-and-miniskirt couples looking to swing, flaunting their gym-toned bodies and making eyes at each other and finger-fucking under the rail with startling candor. Pros from Vegas showed up, as well. Gorgeous but eerily silent twentysomethings in low-cut gowns and Chanel No. 5, sipping Lucien rosé by the glass and waiting with veiled and smoky eyes for one of those same businessmen to get lonely enough to pony up a thousand bucks for a night's company.

A certain lasciviousness seems parcel to wealth, though, or perhaps simply to pool in places of wealth's conspicuousness. Because while he was certainly no Tom Cruise, even Mr. Brooks managed to regularly finagle his way into dalliances with women who really should've known better. In fact, one of the assistant managers—married, a mother, and two decades Mr. Brooks's junior—lost her job after the security team spied a steamy assignation via a closed-circuit TV monitor in a back stairwell. And while Mr. Brooks surely knew why this woman was fired, and though he must've realized everyone had heard the rumors, to my knowledge he never even so much as acknowledged her sudden absence, let alone showed any contrition for the damage caused by his priapic goatiness.

And let's not forget the buxom young Italian woman who sat down across from me one afternoon only to order a Lusty Lady (vodka-cranberry topped with prosecco), a dozen oysters on the half-shell, and a full-size spaghetti and meatball dinner. An unusual repast, to say the least. She drained the cocktail and sucked down the oysters before the pasta was even done boiling. The following evening, she returned to the lounge with a friend—a scantily dressed Latina Betty Boop. Together, they sashayed through the well-heeled crowd, turning heads with their pouty red lips and long bare legs and kohl-thick lashes. Once at the bar, they started in again with the oysters and vodka routine, giggling and making a show of mispronouncing all the menu items ("Char-cut-er-ee? Lard-ons?"). Then, while I was preoccupied stirring an order of drinks, the Italian held her iPhone up to my face.

A video was playing. The volume was low, but I could faintly hear milk splashing from the tub as she and Ms. Boop frolicked in the buff in a luxury suite upstairs.

"I knew there had to be something interesting happening in this hotel," I said.

She smirked and put the phone away and finally admitted that having sex in all that milk wasn't particularly enjoyable. Then she winked at her friend, who'd leaned over to better display the glorious swell of her honey-brown décolletage. "It really makes you think about where it comes from," she added.

Later that same evening, this story having spread like heat rash, Kolcinski—who a few months later would quit to sell real estate full-time, only to grudgingly return when his moneyed connections ghosted him—Googled the Italian woman's name from her credit card receipt. From this, her stage name was quickly deduced, and I have reason to suspect a few Four Seasons employees may have perused her cinematic performances on the sly. In fact, the next day,

Miguel, our Spanish bar manager, asked me if the rumors were true. I asked what rumors he might be referring to and, by way of clarification, he said, "Did you hook up with dat porno star? The one with de oysters."

His thick accent gave the words a weird gravitas.

"Who do you think I am, Mr. Brooks?"

He came around behind the bar, real estate he normally did his best to avoid. "You must be afraid of . . . how you say—fraternizing with de guests?"

I thought of beautiful Miliani out in Hawai'i, starstruck and shit-canned for fraternizing with Tom Cruise. Fame, sex, power, money. Be it Touchstone Pictures or Pornhub.com, maybe it all boiled down to the same lousy transaction? Then Miguel demonstrated how to make our latest menu addition, a sugary blend of citrus vodka and mango sorbet dolloped with a sinker float of Midori, the color scheme meant to mimic the logo of World Cup Brazil.

I strawed a taster; the sugariness left my molars aching. "Well, it looks great," I said. "The colors are spot on."

"Yes, I know," Miguel said, "es awful. But these rich assholes cannot tell a rotten cocktail from Châteauneuf-du-Pape. So long as we charge big money, they happy as clams."

"As oysters, you mean?"

"Whatever," Miguel said.

≈

In *Cocktail*, the symbol of the American Dream, be it the novel's rotten version or the sunnier and crowd-pleasing one of the film, is a bottle of Louis XIII cognac, a luxury distillate described in the film as fifty-years-old, but that actually contains vintage strains of eaux-de-vie upwards of a century old. A standard 750 milliliter bottle runs well north of three-thousand-dollars and the decanter it comes in— solid baccarat crystal adorned with fleur-de-lis and worth hundreds of dollars even when empty—arrives not in a box, but a velvet-lined red coffin.

In both book and film, Brian Flanagan loses a bet to Doug Coughlin, and thus has to bring his old chum a bottle of this stuff. Also in both versions, Coughlin—a career bartender and "aristocrat of the working class"—has seemingly made good by marrying well, only to see his money-making schemes go belly-up.

At one point, Coughlin of the novel riffs on the triumph of materialism. "We can luxuriate in our greed again . . ." he explains. "The Robber Barons are back." And then immediately thereafter is raised the specter of old "Louis Treize," that symbol of conspicuous consumption, proof if ever proof was needed that, as

Coughlin puts it, the New Dealers and Fair Dealers had blown it and disdain for wealth was no longer fashionable.

The Coughlin of the film is played by the Australian actor Bryan Brown, and without his charismatic performance *Cocktail* would fall apart entirely—assuming it doesn't fall apart entirely even despite his charismatic performance. Coughlin is a tough guy, worldly and world-weary, a lothario going to seed, and both the moral voice of the immoral bar world as well as a dire warning for Young Flanagan as to just what awaits if he doesn't make his own bar, Cocktails & Dreams, a reality.

This cinematic Coughlin shares the bottle of Louis XIII with Brian, only to later kill himself in a bout of financial despair. Reading his wry suicide note, Brian weeps.

The Coughlin of the novel, however, has already killed himself (and his young wife) by shotgun when Brian shows up. Hearing the news, Brian struggles not to laugh and drinks the cognac all by himself.

These mirrored endings have much to say about America and the pressures she puts on people, or so it seems to me, especially in light of what I saw and experienced at Four Seasons Seattle. One afternoon in particular comes to mind. I was busy pouring drinks when suddenly there was a commotion: just outside the hotel, above the steep concrete steps leading down toward Alaskan Way and the waterfront, a disturbed man was threatening to jump. A crowd had gathered, some surely trying to talk him down, not that I could hear anything from my glassy perch up in the bar.

My angle wasn't good on what was transpiring, at least not until the man shuffled out onto the ledge overlooking the steps, a twenty-five or thirty-foot drop. He was pale and had a short haircut, dressed in blue-gray clothes, layers and piles of clothes, and he never took his hands from his pockets—not even in those last moments, when his posture stiffened strangely and his knees locked and he tipped headfirst off the high wall.

While I was spared having to see where he landed, I did witness the resulting cleanup. First the police and EMTs, then a pair of Four Seasons employees, a security guard and a porter, spraying down the steps with a hose.

As happy hour wore on, the leaper was the talk of the lounge. While sipping their Manhattans and French 75s and washing down their Kumamotos and Bluepoints with twenty-dollar glasses of whatever Loire Valley pouilly-fumé was currently in vogue, the clientele said all the obligatory things—*how awful, what a shame, mental illness*—although a few of them, a few cocktails in, began cracking the sort of ghoulish jokes that can only be excused when one recalls that death respects not the income bracket.

But then Mr. Brooks strolled in, pink-cheeked and healthy in a gray power suit and crimson tie as if dressed for a Coug reunion. He gazed around the lounge, his domain, his living room, and frowned. "What's the deal? Did something happen?"

"A leaper," I said.

"No kidding, somebody jumped?" He craned his neck, straining to see out the window.

But by this time, I was already pouring his MGD 64 into a frosted glass.

"Extra cold?" Mr. Brooks asked, settling onto his preferred stool.

"This is about as cold as it gets, Mr. Brooks," I said.

<hr/>

A few weeks later, I dragged myself in at eleven a.m., bed-headed and cropsick, the siren song of barley and rye still trumpeting in my blood from the night before, only to be instantly sprung upon by a harried waitress who'd been buffaloed by drink orders from an earlier-than-usual but nasty-as-ever brunch crowd.

Normally, maltreatment at the hands of waitresses didn't bother me much. I was a slow bartender, a plodder, but also one who didn't really care if guests had to wait for their drinks, let alone if waitresses were upset. I'd accepted all of this about myself long ago, in bars far, far away. But I was off my game that morning, hungover enough to be sensitive and vulnerable, and as I went about the first of my opening duties—which was to remove the bottle of Louis XIII from the locked cupboard where it slept at night— that waitress bowled up behind me and shouted: "Where are those goddamn Bloody Marys for table six?"

Startled, I fumbled the bottle. And perhaps this was not unlike the bobbling and fumbling which surely must've occurred when Tom Cruise and Bryan Brown were practicing their bottle magic in the lead up to *Cocktail*—but they definitely hadn't been tossing bottles of Louis.

The decanter hit the floor, half on the mat, half on the tile, and the stopper and neck were crudely guillotined. Half the cognac glugged out before I'd even wiped the sleep from my eyes. The waitress had stomped off, not having noticed this insane havoc and destruction she'd wrought. After ensuring no other witnesses, I picked up that fallen monarch and pondered the ambrosia wafting up from the filthy hex-cut mats as the Jacobins had once pondered the coppery smell of royal blood pooling at Place de le Révolution.

I thought of the end of *Cocktail*, both novel and film, and how this bottle figured in. But reality had imitated history that morning, not art: another King Louis had lost his head. Held to the light, shards of crystal glinted in what cognac hadn't spilled. A total loss.

This was not just a hairy mistake, however, but almost certainly a fireable offense. While not nearly as scandalous as frolicking with Mr. Brooks on closed-circuit TV (let alone with Tom Cruise on Instagram), it was simply too expensive a blunder to ever be forgiven. Management may have waited a month or two by way of documenting my various other demerits—of which there were plenty—so as to couch my dismissal in terms acceptable to HR, but I was toast.

After weighing my options and mulling over the state of my bank account, I came up with a plan. First, I double-strained the surviving cognac through a swatch of cheesecloth to filter out the glass. Then, in the empty manager's office, I found what I knew would be there: an equally empty crystal decanter of the same stuff awaiting return to the distributor for refund credit. Back behind the bar once more (after pouring a healthy dollop into my coffee mug), I topped old Louis Treize off from a thirty-dollar bottle of Hennessy, polished him up, and returned him to his accustomed throne beside the TV.

As the weeks passed, an occasional pour was ordered. That regal bottle ceremoniously brought down, meted out in a polished jigger, warmed in a snifter lain sideways across a cup of steaming water, and finally served with that air of quiet grandeur befitting those willing and able to pay the equivalent of my monthly rent for a thimbleful of liquor.

No one noticed the fraud, of course. Miguel had been right: so long as the pollution was sufficiently gilded, it passed for luxury. Because the point of ordering Louis XIII was not to taste one the world's finest cognacs, but to see the awe of mammon light in the eyes of bartenders and waiters and one's fellow imbibers. A status symbol, yes, but a distinctly libacious one. A swirl of power, a sniff of green, a quaff of envy.

When I look back now on my time at Four Seasons Seattle, I think of that broken bottle and all it seemed to imply, and I think of the Hammering Man tirelessly pounding away across the glitz of First Avenue, and I think of the Skid Road, both the historic route and the route I walked to work each day. These thoughts lead to thoughts of how a century of logging and milling and building, of yearning and planning and striving, has born a tech economy nakedly hostile to the working class, hopelessly gentrified neighborhoods, Pomeranians pampered with lemon drop martinis, and hotels stocked with three-thousand-dollar bottles of booze. All of which brings me full circle, back to the words of Heywood Gould, whose years behind the oak taught him a thing or two about dispossession and alienation, about feeling as if you're on the flipside of the cultural clock, as if one's very life had been somehow rendered a digression, a departure from that essential dream, the one that serves to mask the realities of life and death in the vast American underclass: "Go out into the street and look at the world we've left. Go . . ."

13

DARK SUNGLASSES

Though I've tried to show the humorous side of my experiences traveling and tending bar, to balance out the pathos as a dash of simple syrup balances a cocktail's acidity, not all the portraits I might sketch are quite so lighthearted. The people weren't all fun-loving whiskey boys like Korean Schwarzenegger, or wisecracking bar vets like Frank O'Brien, full of one-liners and tongue-in-cheek lessons about Halfers and Service Chicken. No, there was darkness there, too. Plenty of it. The industry is rough on people, the work exhausting both physically and psychologically, and each night behind the oak can come to seem like just one more stop on the way to an emotional dead-end. And when my thoughts turn down such paths, I inevitably recall a certain young woman—one who, when they finally saw fit to discharge her, was pale and silent and had these raccoonishly gray rings around her eyes, as if from a long night of boozing. But while she dearly loved her Irish whiskey, her Bushmills and her Red Breast, this was no hangover.

We'd first met at Four Seasons Seattle, stirring cocktails for Mr. and Mrs. Brooks and the rest of the uppity crowd, and soon enough we were meeting up after work to vent our frustrations and make fun of those very same customers over shots and late-night burgers at a nearby French bistro—a bistro just down the stairs from where that homeless man leapt. There'd been instant chemistry between us, like spirits poured over crackling ice. And I suppose I'd been ready for someone like her, someone fresh and full of life, being not long removed from that lonely stint on Lana'i. But while we'd clung to each other, I soon dumped the hotel gig in favor of pulling taps at a craft beer hideout near the University District.

So, try and picture me there a few months later, melancholy and distracted, on a lazy Sunday during fresh hop season, those drizzly days of late autumn. A handful of locals quietly sip ale and stare forlornly at their iPhones while a Seahawks game plays on the TV sans volume.

Then in walk two middle-aged Asian guys, one of whom is blind. He reads the floor with the tip of his cane, tap, tap, tap, just like the raindrops. After taking stools, they order a round of Chimay. We introduce ourselves, agree that the Seahawks aren't quite as good as last year, and then the conversation takes a strange turn.

"Guess," says the friend to the blind man, "what our bartender looks like?"

A pair of dark sunglasses rotate my way. The man grins and tips his head back, showing twin horseshoes of small dull teeth. It's the exact pose of Ray Charles at the piano and I wonder about the connection, whether the overpowering nature of sight causes us to genuflect and renounce our human instinct to face the heavens. His fingers grope for the beer goblet. I resist the urge to slide it closer, to baby him.

"He is very tall," the blind man says. His friend laughs and says yes, yes, he is quite tall. But the blind compensate via acute hearing, don't they? He might've easily discerned my voice came from higher up than normal.

"And he is not bad looking," the blind man adds.

A reasonable appearance is guessable, too, considering my role in the service industry. But how might this little act go if I were a female bartender—what was their play?

I think of "Cathedral" by Ray Carver, a story about blindness and booze and different ways of seeing. I don't mention it, of course, as it'd be rude to compare a man's real-life disability to fiction. Still, the story imbues the moment. But the blind man's Cheshire grin never wavers. He is nonfiction. He rocks slowly to and fro, not to the Mad Season track pounding over the stereo, but to some private melody all his own. His cane falls against an adjacent stool with a gentle *thock*.

"What else?" says his companion. "What else do you see?"

Intentional or otherwise, they've managed to create a pocket of tension. It's like we really are in a Carver story, or like we're about to hear the straight dope from the *bodhisattva*. Are they brothers? Friends? Con men? A waitress, a busboy, and the pasty and morose couple three stools down all eavesdrop now. There's something fascinating about the blind. A sense of the oracular. Tiresias and Oedipus, Eli, Jesus spitting and rubbing and laying on hands, and finally the milky eggs lurking behind those darkened shades just across the oak. I try to imagine the terrible freedom that must accompany such a loss but can't. Not really.

Finally, the blind man claps his hands. "And the barman," he says, "is unlucky in love."

A drink ticket chattered out of the printer just then, breaking the weird spell, and everyone shared an awkward laugh. Everyone except for me, that is. Because I was seeing not dark sunglasses, but exhausted gray rings around a pair of soft blue eyes. There'd been a troubling phone call just before midnight followed by a panicked and rainslick drive across the city. Then a lightless and half-renovated boarding house, a closed door, a spill of empty prescription bottles on a ratty mauve carpet, and then her familiar body in my arms, weightless as a dove as my clumsy feet pounded down a spiral staircase full of bent nails.

Unlucky in love?

This is why I don't put much stock in prophecy. Because looking back on what happened, on that night and all the other nights, both those before and after, I do feel lucky—very lucky—to have found her when I did.

14

HAPPY HOUR IN AN ITALIAN RESTAURANT

Tucked away alongside an unremarkable suburban road somewhere north of Seattle was an Italian restaurant and leading up to its front door was an elaborate iron trellis and from that trellis hung an open sign, the neon letters stuttering, flickering, fading. Inside, thick shades blocked out the late afternoon sun, and the ruby light from the hanging fixtures was dim—so dim that one might fail to notice the peeling varnish on the bar or the crumbs of desiccated food on the threadbare carpet or the cobwebs and dust adorning the dark and stoppered bottles along the back wall. If the regulars noticed the decay, however, no one said anything. In fact, it was as if they saw the restaurant the way it'd been in the past, before the long, slow decline.

Sitting at bar's end, in the dusky shadows under the muted television, was Lily. She'd owned the place since the nineties, but she'd only come to run it in the last few years, since her husband ran off to Maui with a regular. Her wine glass was empty, but I knew better than to ask whether she might like another. Although she'd hired me to tend bar, she preferred to pour her own, so as to preserve certain necessary illusions. Lily was tall and redheaded, her eyes a watery blue. The skin of her face was blossomed with worrisome constellations of small red stars and veins, but that she'd once been a strikingly beautiful woman was obvious to all. Lily also had something of a tragic past. Besides the absentee husband, she'd lost a son some years back, while another son was recently home after a spell in rehab down in L. A.

Three stools over was Benny, nursing a scotch and soda while staring at the TV, a last few wisps of white hair floating around his scalp like spun threads of cotton candy. In time, he'd order another scotch and soda, and then he'd have a glass of the house red before happy hour ended. Benny had recently suffered a stroke, and this shortly after becoming a widower. The accumulated blows had left him fragile and prone to lose the thread of conversation. He was also estranged from his only son and occasionally got a little tipsy and called me by that son's name (a mix-up I never dared acknowledge, let alone correct). As usual, Benny was waiting for his friend Dennis, a potbellied bore with kidney trouble who tipped in quarters and cadged food from other people's plates. But at Benny's age a man hasn't much choice in friends.

Except for the Spanglish chattering of Freddy and Norberto back in the kitchen—brothers, Norberto cooked while Freddy prepped and washed dishes—and Sinatra's olive-oil crooning on the stereo, the restaurant could've been a mausoleum. I polished a wine glass and sat it on the backbar: a faint clink on the faux marble.

The quiet was soon interrupted, though, as Hannah burst through the kitchen's back door in a flouncy rush. She waitressed six nights a week, her two-year-old son watched over by her dad and stepmom. The boy's father was her high school sweetheart, now serving three-to-five on meth charges. Hannah had seemingly given up on him—she had a series of other men in her life—but she did take their son on penitentiary visits every so often. I tried my best to see Hannah as the hardworking single mother that she truly was, but she had a way of making it difficult. Freddy, on the other hand, was in love. Soon came the sound of his broken English and Hannah shrieking at whatever flirty thing he'd said—"Freddy, stop! Shut *up*, Freddy!"

Down the rail, Lily's eyes flicked toward the noise. Hannah's antics got under Lily's skin, but Lily sympathized with the girl's situation, and besides (as everyone said), Hannah was "good with the customers," which meant that she could be charming in thirty-second intervals, just long enough to take a drink order and suggest the calamari. Then Lily was up and around the bar, rooting in the fridge for an icy bottle of Sonoma-Cutrer. Benny watched her refill her glass, but it was as if his eyes had settled upon her without actually seeing, like he was caught in a waking dream.

Shortly afterward, Dennis showed up, gray and gloaming as ever. He smirked at me as if something about my presence amused him. This despite the fact that I was the only staff member with whom he remained on speaking terms. Regardless, I poured his usual gimlet, fishing the canister of sour mix from where it floated beside the kegs in a puddle of bilge water. I stuck a days-old and gummy lime wedge on the rim and pushed the cocktail across the bar. When Dennis asked how I was doing, I said fine. But when I returned the question, he ignored me and commenced bragging to Benny about his stock portfolio.

Later, while I was mixing Benny's second scotch and soda, a man I'd never seen before walked in and approached the bar. He asked for a table in the dining room. He was in his mid-fifties and dressed in gym clothes—baggy shorts with a pale blue wrinkled T-shirt and white Nikes. His jaws were rough and gray, his blondish hair uncombed. There was something about his eyes, though. A drubbed emptiness. I wondered if he'd been drinking already.

I asked if anyone would be joining him, but he just shook his head.

So, I grabbed a menu and wine list and led him past the open kitchen and into the empty dining room. It was early still. There likely wouldn't be another table for an hour or more.

He took a seat where I suggested, near the wine cage and with his back against the thin partition that separated the dining room from the prep area, the cramped little stretch where salads were plated, coffee brewed, silverware polished and rolled. Although he was Hannah's customer, I went ahead and asked if he'd like a cocktail or a glass of wine. He looked up at me then, as if my words hadn't quite registered. Like Benny, he seemed to gaze past the restaurant and into some other and far distant place.

Finally, he blinked. "A red, maybe?"

I rattled off our selections by the glass, merlots and cabs, Chianti and sangiovese and nebbiolo, but again I had the odd sense that the man wasn't fully registering my presence, that he heard something other than the sound of my voice. Finally, he just pointed at the list.

Back at the bar, I poured a glass of zinfandel, vaguely irritated to find myself doing Hannah's job (she was still in the kitchen, chowing down on whatever special dish Freddy had whipped up), but upon returning to the man's table, I found him in tears.

I waited to present the wine. Once he'd noticed me, I asked if everything was all right.

"It's my mother," he said, and then dried his face on a black linen napkin.

I said I was sorry and asked if the woman was ill.

"She's gone," he said. "My mom died—just an hour ago."

I cannot now remember what I said to him, although I must've said something. What I do recall is that when I placed the zin on the table, just a few inches from his hands, those hands were trembling. I promised to send his waitress right over.

After a search, I finally found Hannah outside the kitchen's back door, texting and vaping. Like always, she'd pancaked her face with makeup and mascara and dark lipstick. She had a new tattoo on her forearm, as well, although I couldn't decipher the scrolling and reddened gothic letters. I told her what I'd learned of her latest customer.

"Wait, his mom died—and he came *here?*"

Ignoring this, I told her he'd already ordered wine and was planning to have a meal, as well. "You really should do something nice for him," I said. "Comp that wine, or maybe give him a gelato or tiramisu on the house."

"But Lily is still here," Hannah said.

"It's just a couple bucks. Lily will understand."

"Okay, whatever."

"And Hannah—don't let on that I said anything. That wouldn't be good."

"Duh," she said, and went back to texting.

At the bar once again, I explained the situation to Lily. As I spoke, the soft skin of her face seemed to soften even more. That glass of chardonnay still clutched in her hands, she glanced back at the entrance to the dining room, although she couldn't see the man's table from there. But just before Lily began to speak, her son drifted in. He was skinny and had a complexion like cottage cheese, his hair an oily mop. And though he was dressed for work in black on black (the plan was to bus tables while figuring out school), within moments of giving his mother a hug and clocking in, he disappeared into the restroom; the sound of the bolt turning echoed down the length of the darkened hallway.

Later, while being chastised by Dennis for using too much ice and mix in his second cocktail, Maureen came in. She was about Lily's age, a devotee of blue jeans and loudly printed shirts and sweaters. She also loved cats. So much so that she volunteered at the local animal shelter; so much so that she tended to bring cats with her wherever she went. The carrier was swathed in a thick purple blanket but still, you could hear the soprano mewlings of its cargo.

"Maureen," Lily said, "you know you can't bring them in here."

But this was a familiar routine and soon enough both women were pulling fuzzy kittens from the carrier, petting and cooing. Across the room, Norberto smirked and shook his head, mixing gnocchi or maybe stirring marinara on the far side of the pass-through amidst tendrils of steam rising from cauldrons of boiling pasta. He raised a finger to his temple and twirled it.

Benny had noticed, too. Having turned slowly on his stool, he said, "Well Dennis, will you look at that . . . Maureen brought kittens . . ."

"Cats are idiots," Dennis said, and pushed his cocktail across the bar, staring at me as he did so. But instead of remixing the drink, I walked away. In the kitchen, I found Hannah still texting. I asked what the man in the dining room had ordered.

She glanced up as if unsure who or what I was referring to. "Clams linguine," she finally said, and was about to head back outside again when I reminded her to take a little something off his bill, or at least keep checking on him, to make him feel cared for. She gave me her serious face and promised she would, but then Freddy rounded the corner carrying a big loaf of fresh-baked ciabatta. He saw us and then flashed a grin full of metal bridgework. "Hannah Banana," he said, "es muy bonita . . . es mi novia . . . mi esposa . . . es la madre para mis hijos . . ."

"Freddy! Shut *up!*"

At the bar I found Lily quietly weeping. Maureen had taken the stool beside her (with the cat carrier occupying the stool beside that) and was rubbing Lily's back and whispering into her ear. Down the rail, Dennis had gone still, apparently under the misapprehension that stillness made his eavesdropping less obvious, while Benny remained as he'd been all afternoon, content to stare at the flickering ghosts on the silent television.

"Now about this cocktail . . ." Dennis said, but again I ignored him. While I actually didn't want to eavesdrop, it was clear Lily was talking about her son—who was still mysteriously locked in the men's room—and that Maureen was doing her best to be a good friend. This too I'd seen before. I made a sipping motion at Maureen and, still pampering Lily, she mouthed the word *cabernet*.

As I poured, Maureen reached into the carrier, this time pulling out an unusually handsome kitten—a longhaired tabby with shining white boots and a luxurious cravat to match. She rolled the creature around in her lap, baby-talking it, and soon enough Lily, though still weepy, was petting those tufted ears and that soft belly and jaunty little tail.

Then the bell dinged in the pass-through, Norberto having put the finishing touches on the clam linguine, sprinkling the rich broth with parsley. Hannah was nowhere in sight. I gave her a minute, but still she didn't show. Annoyed, Norberto smacked the bell again, harder. I was around the bar and halfway there when Hannah burst through the swinging door from the prep area. She had food in her mouth. "Got it!" she called out, still chewing, and snatched the steaming bowl from the window.

Watching her hustle into the dining room, bracelets ajangle, I thought of the man who'd lost his mother. Why had he chosen this restaurant—was it a place the two of them had dined together? Or had he just stumbled in at random, the short-circuited open sign blinking off and on like a beacon in a dark sea? I thought of my own mother then, who was in her late seventies and lived thousands of miles away. I imagined those inevitable moments after—strangers behaving as if nothing whatsoever had happened, the night rolling on, people drinking wine and putting spaghetti into their mouths while looking at television sets.

Twenty minutes later, I poured Benny his familiar glass of red and then walked back into the dining room. I headed for the wine cage and pretended to search for a bottle. From the corner of my eye, I could see the man had pushed his dinner aside, having barely picked at it. The wine I'd poured was largely untouched, as well. As I passed back by his table, I cleared the dish, hoping he might take to the opportunity to speak again, to confide something that might help in some small way, or give me an opportunity to do the same. But he didn't. He merely sat there, staring at the empty tablecloth.

Hannah was in the prep area, joking with Freddy and clumsily sawing bread. I showed her the bowl of clams and pasta.

She looked at me wide-eyed. "He didn't like it?"

Freddy grinned and tossed a lump of dough into a container. "Hannah es mi amor..."

I told her the man seemed ready for his check, but before I dropped the bowl in the dish pit, I reminded her yet again to comp his wine. "I don't think he wants dessert, but just do something special for him—"

Then the bread knife slid across the hardened crust and nicked Hannah's finger. She swore and raised her voice: "What? Homeboy's mom dies and so now I'm supposed to go suck his dick?"

And just then the track happened to change on the stereo, from Sinatra to something else, and the steady clatter of Freddy and Norberto's cooking and dishwashing happened to fall into that same beat of silence, as did the voices from the bar, and perhaps even some low mechanical hum—ventilation, a clacking fridge, the tick of a food timer, that collective white noise of the working restaurant. The partition separating the dining room was thin, more flimsy curtain than actual wall. In the long moment after, Hannah and I both stared at that spot where, just on the other side, the bereaved man still sat.

"Hannah Banana..." Freddy said, still grinning and portioning out his dough, "es mi chica..."

Not long afterward, while I stood behind the bar polishing rocks glasses that needed no further polishing, the man emerged from the dining room. He stood in the entranceway, still as a stone in his rumpled gym clothes, until he finally caught my eye; and then he didn't let it go, not with each of the dozen steps he took toward the exit. It wasn't an aggressive look he gave me, though, nor even angry. It was something else, something worse, and I found myself unable to glance away, not when Dennis demanded his check, not when Lily slurrily asked whether anyone had seen her son, not even when one of Maureen's kittens wriggled free and dashed down the oak, its tail bumping and nearly spilling the remains of Benny's happy hour red.

Even before the door had bumped softly closed in the man's wake, I knew I'd someday write about him. That I'd take his story and fold it into my own. That what was perhaps the worst day of his life would become just another lonely bar tale. And I didn't—and still really don't—know quite how to feel about that.

15

IN A HEAP

As a longtime bartender, I've often heard the hangover described in colorful terms—brown bottle 'flu and a case of the old bottle ache, in a heap and red-eyed, cropsick and crapulent, fur-tongued and katzenjammered (of Germanic origin; evoking the wailing of cats)—all of which is reminiscent of how Jackson's *The Lost Weekend* describes the hangover's "hilarious vocabulary . . . the jitters, the ginters, the booze-blues . . . the moaning after." But as a skilled purveyor of the source of this jargon-rich malady, I've often been consulted as to the effectiveness of a series of superstitious and frequently rhyming preventatives: beer before liquor never been sicker; liquor before beer and you're in the clear; clear liquor over brown; lager over ale; sleep with one foot planted firmly on the floor to halt the spinning; and so on.

None of these methods actually work, I'm afraid, and yet hope of an easy fix persists. The committed drinker will blame his mornings after on virtually anything: the sugar in the mixers, the tannins in the wine, the congeners in the bourbon—the time of day, the weather, even their mood prior to imbibing. What's less often mentioned, however, is the hangover's relationship to time. Because make no mistake, what fills those shapely bottles is poison—lovely poisons for which the only surefire antidote is the passage of the hours.

I should know, as I've sacrificed many an hour in just this way. And though I'm agnostic as a dung beetle, the suffering and regret almost inescapably suggests Catholicism: sin, guilt, repentance, and finally confession, most often whispered to the bottom of a garbage can or toilet bowl. A penance paid for allowing the id to outfox the ego, for attempting to exercise courage one doesn't actually possess, to drown and thereby escape our due inheritance of anxiety. Or perhaps these raw and headachy mornings are actually more akin to Buddhism? After all, if the essence of our existence is indeed suffering, it's feasible this entire go-around has been nothing but a hangover from a previous life's bender, as if the reincarnated soul were a candlewick soaked with bonded bourbon lit from another earlier wick soaked in Bacardi 151.

But my first hangover was definitely Protestant. Early in my freshman year of high school, a pair of Baptist preacher's kids threw a beer bash when their parents left town. Our fuel was Bud Ice, a swill most foul produced by freezing regular Budweiser and skimming off the ice crystals, thereby boosting the ethanol percentage. Deep into the evening and ten cans down, I placed my hand on the blue-jeaned hip of a girl named Holly. Holly was always friendly and had a tendency to show up wherever I was hanging out, but she was also a couple of years older, a junior, a veritable woman, and so I'd never before found the courage to think of her romantically—and but for the Bud Ice, I likely never would have. After considering my bibulous state, however, Holly gently removed my hand from her hip and suggested I get some sleep.

Come morning, the preacher's daughter gave me a lift home. Shivery and pale, I took a few steps across the yard before collapsing in the grass just shy of the front porch. I remained there curled and retching for a solid hour. Somehow, my parents failed to notice.

My hangovers continued like this, infrequent and largely comedic, until at some point their frequency and tone changed. No longer an intermittent and harmless bottle 'flu, but a malaise and amnesia that might last for days—and yet the suffering of these bouts did little to inhibit my further drinking. College friends often pointed out that nobody else could drink like me, and I swallowed this praise, pounding beers and shooting whiskey, but even then a part of me heard it differently: no one else *does* or *would* drink like me. As Carol Knapp writes in her memoir, *Drinking: A Love Story,* this difference between myself and other people, insofar as I could never quite seem to get enough booze, whereas they had a natural stopping point, is evidence of a disease—of alcoholism, or at least the potential for it. And there was the more practical, day-to-day evidence: I failed tests and missed essay deadlines and was fired from an early morning job at the athletic center after snoring through my very first shift. I also began incurring strange injuries, a lacerated scalp, a broken toe, horrible ankle sprains and mysterious bruising from half-remembered falls. My personality darkened, as well, as if all that alcohol pouring in were bleaching away youth's optimism.

One morning near the end of my freshman year, I woke with a fat lip and swollen right hand. The night before came swimming back. A friend and I were on the edge of campus talking to some young women we knew, when three guys approached from the direction of the local bars. For whatever reason, I made eye contact with one of them; he wouldn't look away and so, naturally, neither would I. Then he flicked his cigarette at my chest. After I told him what I thought of that, he came at me with his fists balled and his chin thrust out. So, I slugged him in that same chin. It was the first time I'd ever done such a thing and the punch was tentative, more a stern but experimental clubbing. Then one of his friends blindsided me and busted my lip, though I can't recall it hurting very much. Later, an X-ray confirmed a cracked fifth metacarpal, but I merely joked that my boxer's fracture was a good excuse to hold a frosty can of beer.

Sophomore year, I came to one night at the witching hour, disturbed by the sound of someone trying the locked door to my room. I rose from the couch, foggy and disoriented, and stood in the yellowy wash from the streetlamp just outside my second story window. Then my phone rang. "Don't answer your door, man," said the guy from down the hall. I retracted my hand from the insistently jiggling knob, and listened as my concerned neighbor explained that a group of guys were trying to break in. "One of them has a baseball bat," he added.

Hours earlier, amidst the sweaty chaos of a basement keg party, I'd crossed paths with a football player everyone called Big Pete. He had a reputation as the campus tough guy, a bad drunk, a coke-head and steroid-abuser. Pete was far beefier and stronger than me and, frightened, I'd tried to walk away. But the party was crowded and he followed, pushing me in the center of my back and growling weird threats. I remember how red and slitted his eyes were and how all I wanted was to be away from him, away from the blaring hip-hop and crush of bodies. But for whatever reason Pete had singled me out. Lanky and baby-faced, I must've looked like an easy target. But Pete had no way of knowing the cocktail of fear and anger and hurt I carried around inside of me, and so he underestimated the possibility of my hurting back.

After yet another unprovoked shove, I spun and hit him in the face as hard as I could. My hand didn't break this time, but Pete's nose certainly did. Somehow, he kept his feet, looking more shocked than injured. But then he yanked back his huge arm to throw a punch of his own—in turn smashing bloody the face of an unsuspecting young woman standing behind him—and so I hit him again in the gory red mess of his nose. Then other guys were shouting and pushing, separating us. I felt sick in the wake of it, shaky and wrung-out, and I can still remember the blood. Blood on Pete's clothing, on my knuckles, on the muddy and beer-streaked floor.

Alone in my dorm that night, having groggily processed my neighbor's warning, I pretended to call campus security, shouting into the receiver so my would-be assailants heard my voice through the door. In the days to come, people warned me that I needed to watch my back, maybe even leave school for a while, that Big Pete and his football friends were gunning for me. Sure enough, a few weeks later my car was found totaled in an empty parking lot, tires flattened and hood stomped in and every last one of its windows shattered. When the police called to ask if I knew of anyone who might be holding a grudge, I thought of that baseball bat and played dumb, as I'd apparently gotten off easy, all things considered.

Junior year, I awoke one morning with vague memories of arguing with my girlfriend, one who thought she loved me, but who also wanted to fix me, collar me, save me. In the filthy bathroom down the hall, I fell to my knees and stuck my finger down my throat, as if to purge the memory of the night before, when I'd heard my father's ugly words—words I'd sworn I would never use on another person, words that sounded uncannily like his vicious and constant fights with my mother—come roaring out of my own mouth and into that confused girl's weeping face. And in the decades to come, I remember all the bedrooms of all the young women I awoke in, queasy with the knowledge that another young woman lay alone somewhere in the city (in whichever city it happened to be), wondering where I'd gone and who I was with and why I couldn't quite seem to love her back.

Or the early afternoon at age twenty-six, when I finally roused from a narcotic sleep only to recall my car had been impounded the night before. I'd been driving home from a bar when suddenly my rearview was flooded with red and blue strobes. The window sinking into the door and a flashlight in my face, my pupils black and round as vinyl LPs. I recall standing alongside the road and struggling to follow a pen light with my eyes, such desperate concentration, the night wind whipping my shirt around my ribs. The older and grayer of the two officers oversaw the investigation while his young partner demonstrated the last of the tests, something to do with counting while standing on one foot—only just then he lost his balance and stumbled down the incline upon which I'd happened to pull over. The older officer shook his head and looked back at the cruiser, as if picturing the botched investigation on the rolling dash-cam.

They called for an impound truck and stuffed me uncuffed into the back of the cruiser, my certain arrest and conviction spoiled by the happenstance of a hill and gravity and a few small, slippery rocks. During the ride, the older officer spoke to me, his voice low and tired, his eyes catching mine in the rearview: *I* know you honestly don't think you're drunk—somebody just like you tells me that every night—but I can smell you from here.

So it went: more bad decisions, more wasted opportunities, and more breakups (always easier to yank the Band-Aid in the morning's nauseous half-light), as well as more blackouts and more fights, including the morning I awoke with a thundering headache and a hospital bracelet around my wrist, having been beaten unconscious by two young men after a house party spilled out onto the street.

And let's not forget that morning a few years later, when dawn saw me whiskey-sick and soul-sick from an incident with an estranged older brother, a confrontation decades in the making. I'd been visiting home, and a friend of mine from high school had been driving us around the central Illinois moonscape as we all drank too much beer and bullshitted. Then we stopped for a bladder break. My brother and I stood shoulder to shoulder, watering a ditch, and I made a lame joke of pretending to wet his sneaker. He failed to see the humor. In fact, he clinched his fists and squared his shoulders. But then a whole childhood boiled up inside of me and I shoved him—shoved him harder than I'd meant to—and he catapulted backwards to the hard earth. Seeing him that way, sprawled and dazed, I immediately regretted my actions, regretted our drinking, regretted all that we'd failed to mean to one another. I helped him to his feet and apologized and suggested we call it a night.

Shortly thereafter, trolling through the darkness in my friend's truck, my brother's arm snaked out from the backseat and circled my neck. In his hand was a knife, and in the second before that knife disappeared beneath my chin, its steel glinted sickly green in the dashboard glow. The blade dimpled an artery, cool against my skin. I pressed my head back as far as it would go, but the seatback was unforgiving, and the knife pressed deeper. Then a voice eerily like my own whispered a promise to cut my throat from ear to ear. I risked a glance and saw my brother's face, mere inches away. It too glowed that same sickly green. At one time at least, we'd looked a lot alike, but I didn't recognize him now, not at all, and I was badly frightened.

I shouted over and over for my friend to stop the truck. After a panicked quarter mile, he finally did. Somehow, I managed to talk a little distance between myself and that knife, just enough to slip from the overheated cab. Later, having dropped my brother in town, that friend came back and found me walking the lightless dirt roads. He confessed he'd not known what to do, that the experience had brought back bad memories of having a blade pulled on him in Macedonia, that as I'd shouted for him to stop the truck, he'd feared both the possibility of stepping too hard on the brakes, as well as the prospect of being alone with my brother.

The following day, I'd already put five-hundred miles between myself and my hometown when my mother called to say my brother was in the hospital. In the wake of the fight, he'd initially returned to our childhood home, only to flash that same sharp knife in our father's face while demanding the half-senile old man finally acknowledge and accept responsibility for the emotional wreckage and violence of his drunken sons. But later, back at his apartment, he'd fallen sick and then unconscious. He might have died had a neighbor not found him. In the emergency room, doctors bored a hole in his skull with an electric drill bit by way of relieving the pressure on his brain. A few days later, he sent me a text that read, *if u evr lay hands on me again, u r a ded man.*

It almost could've been the whiskey talking, and yet somehow, I managed to survive my twenties and early thirties, despite the various career and personal mistakes that piled up behind me like a host of emptied bottles. At some point, though, I finally gave up on being someone I wasn't or maybe simply couldn't be. All along I'd been writing, if poorly, if naively, and while that may have looked like failure to others, I was also writing in a way attuned to both the ebb and flow of language and the mystery of words-as-art, and thus a way that allowed for growth. A bad book is only truly bad if it doesn't lead to another, better book. And despite the bad books I'd written, there was a voice there, one struggling to burble up from a dark tarn of booze and exhaustion and frustration. Then, in the years to follow, my father grew ill and mad and infirm, and somewhere over that span of time I ceased to hear his angry voice in my head quite so incessantly, and from that newfound quiet emerged words of my own, and the anger and hurt I'd grown up with and carried with me into young manhood faded into a persistent but gentle melancholy, and so with it the drinking mellowed from torrents and floods to a steady drip.

While I still slip up on occasion and wander too far down the Path of Forgetting, the hangovers have mostly lost their venom. Morning has now transformed into the finest part of the day, a cleansed and meditative set of hours that begin with my easing up from bed, so as not to wake the lovely woman I share it with. Once the coffee is dripping, I read for a while in the house's agreeable quiet and then scribble down whatever words happen to rise. I look at the red cedars beyond the big windows and feed our newly adopted little black tomcat his beloved tuna fish and milk.

I'm forty now, though. Halfway down the rail. And so I've come to see those old hangovers in a different light. Because I lost not just the pleasure of feeling healthy in the morning, and not just friendships and relationships and whatever opportunities I was too red-eyed and cropsick to recognize, but time—at least a decade if not more, and not just due to feeling ill, but to that deeper illness that made me yearn to float at bottle's bottom. That lost time, that "most shameful and wanton waste of all," in Charles Jackson's words, troubles me now. It represents books not read and known, places not traveled and explored, people not met and understood, and other good things missed.

And while fate later saw fit to send Big Pete once more across my path—this time outside a Chicago bar at last call—after a few tense moments, we shared a weird laugh and reminisced about the zany college guys we'd once been, how I'd flattened his nose with my fist and how he'd meant to cave in my skull with an aluminum bat . . . and though that brother and I managed to remain peaceful and relatively sober at our father's funeral, and despite the many rides home I've given to drinkers who've had two too many, whether at my bar or some other bar, so as to keep the midnight roads clear of drivers such as I once was, I suspect there's no way to atone for that other aspect of the hangover.

No, while we may joke about our katzenjammers over brunch, grinning through the misery of our bottle ache, wincing as we sip a screwdriver and stare down that plate of runny eggs and toast, there's nothing all that funny about the realization that some irreplaceable portion of this unique reincarnation has been squandered, forgotten or wasted, drunk.

There's no making amends for that. At least not this go-around.

16

AQUA VITAE

Another dreary wet day in that aimless and dangling week before Christmas and gloom tidings sip at the very marrow of my bones. It's almost as if whatever may have remained of my youthful optimism has sunk deep into the slatted cask of my body, only to be pressed out again by the season's constricting cold, a more nuanced but darker spirit.

It's not the melancholia that ultimately gets you, though; it's the absence of pleasure. More specifically, the suspicion that the old and familiar pleasures are still around somewhere, and yet you've somehow lost the scent for them. Misplaced them in a hall closet or thoughtlessly regifted them to an acquaintance. Because our pleasures are crucial. They're all we have to balance the creeping empty. To convince ourselves, if only for a moment, that the bitter gift is worth it. A cut of beef with carrots and onions simmered in a bourguignon sauce thick and salty as blood. A cold apricot on a day when you'd forgotten just how good that soft, sweet flesh can taste. The sound of a basketball snapping the cords. Those passages from Melville that swell and boom like the heaving of his grandiloquent sea. Roberta Flack on vinyl. A foot rub that lingers along the arch. And sex, of course. That timeless hunt for first love's terra incognita.

On a day such as this, sunless and listless and caroling, the soul clamors for distraction, but for more than that—for solace. Something has to weigh against the gloaming, after all, to collar and restrain the black dog, else the scales will surely tip. Add to the Yuletide season's inherent miseries those daily frustrations that mark the writing life, the doing without, the featureless mask of emotional celibacy, that constant drumbeat of bland food, burned coffee, dim light, a hard chair, a tetchy cat, and the Northwest's lulling gray rain, that numbing pat, pat, pat, drip, drip, drip . . . and what ultimately ends up on the page is not so much a story imbued with the stuff of life, but a string of cold, dead nouns, the listlessness of the drawn out line, literary anhedonia.

So, if the situation is truly as it appears, and Nietzsche was right and God is dead and Camus was right in that all our talk is but a shallow rampart against the logic of self-harm, and if the physicists are right and this galaxy ends in entropic heat death such that not even cinders will remain, and if the behavior of our species can be taken at face value such that our so-called morals and ethics are really just the means by which those without power lessen the sting of having found themselves powerless, then it seems we'd best find a balm that works, and quick.

Hence, single malt.

⁓

A most blunt and startling of facts: my father is no longer living. My father is dead. A strange thing to put on paper, to see in black-and-white and try to recognize as true, but true it is. He died just this past year, and not in the easiest of ways. Shrunken and frail, incontinent and demented, my mother taping notes to the microwave because he couldn't quite recall how to reheat his coffee (1:45, press GO!), and then the fall that finally did him, a steep descent into muteness, ambulance rides, and hospital visits: Can you try to count backwards from one hundred by seven? Who's the president currently? What year were you born? Where *are* we right now?

This will be the first Christmas since. Not that he and I bothered to get together over the holidays, but still. The season has a way of limning such things. But while a Scrooge my father no doubt was, he never quite found his redemption. Whether that was for lack of helpful ghosts, or because he was too busy shouting at the politicians on TV doesn't particularly matter now. I do believe, though, that my father was in his own way a searcher. Two decades ago, for example, when I was barely out of high school, my mother confided that he habitually asked a singularly morose and unanswerable question: "Is this all there is?"

Is *this* all there is?

Is this *all* there is?

Is this all there *is?*

While I never actually heard my father speak the words, and therefore can't deduce anything from inflection, the question seems to carry within it echoes of the meaning of life and God and why something rather than nothing. Of course, it was easier as a kid to scoff at the old man's dark nights of the soul. Easier still to pity my mother, as I sensed in the query an indictment of our lives. As with Walter Murray Gibson on Oahu, my father founded his own small-town newspaper in rural Illinois and threw himself into the venture. His own paper was what he'd always claimed to want, his print-smudged version of the American Dream, and yet there he was saying moony things to his long-suffering wife. Because while his question was no doubt sincere, the answer is patently obvious: yes. Absolutely. It's just this and nothing more. Religions are well-meaning fibs, presumptions of meaning are but thinly veiled defense mechanisms, and altruism is the last refuge of the willfully blind. We're made of chemicals, we come together and dissolve, and it all happens with great swiftness and to no discernible purpose.

The point here, however, is not existential posturing (although when better than Christmastime for that?), but instead to note that the very asking of such a question suggests my father already sensed the answer. And yet he lived otherwise. A shame, too, as his was a very old enquiry and settled long ago. The Epicureans, who flourished in the centuries shortly before Christ, accepted there was no afterlife, just as they understood human existence was marked by great anxiety, confusion, and pain. The answer: to cultivate pleasures. Not gluttony, of course. No Dionysian orgies—or at least not too many. Instead, a person ought to first pare down their needs and wants, thereby limiting their potential for feeling deprived either physically or mentally, and then indulge whatever simple but durable pleasures remain. Good food, pleasant drinks, deep friendships, sex if you must, and all the consolations of philosophy. Herein lay tranquility, or as close to tranquility as we're likely to get in this realm.

For myself, especially as I've gotten older, Epicureanism has seemed both truer and ever more synonymous with one spirit in particular: single malt whiskey. Now I can understand how that may sound flippant given the context here, and yes, I'll take the sex and philosophy, but neither above the malt. For the uninitiated, pure malt is scotch's Platonic form, the idea of what the thing should be. Unlike the blended stuff, single malt is unsullied by grain whiskies, cheap and characterless filler known by the old-timers as "silent spirit" because such distillates spoke nothing of their provenance. Single malts, on the other hand, are a high wine of Scottish barley, smoked by tarry peat and rested in oaken casks for the approximate length of a human adolescence. For my money, there's little better.

Whiskey—or at least any drink we'd recognize as whiskey today—originated in either Scotland or Ireland and derives from the Gaelic *uisce beatha*, which like the Latin *aqua vitae* means "water of life." The Celtic triskele of interlocking spirals, an ancient symbol of nature and mysticism that appears frequently in Christian and pre-Christian art (and in the Irish tchotchke decorating my mother's kitchen, long a gripe of my father), bears striking resemblance to the *viscimetric* whorls of water meeting distillate—those oily and potent fingers that, to borrow a phrase from Neil Gunn, uncurl in the glass like a lingering benediction.

All of this can be no coincidence. We are meant to stare into whiskey's amber depths and feel anew the specific gravity of our existence. But if on occasion we behave less like epicures and more like hedonists, we may find another level, a state capable of mimicking pleasure, a sort of rapturous amnesia that Emerson claims "insulates us in thought, whilst it unites us in feeling." And maybe this haze, this lubricious and ribald moderation of our moderations, is also necessary. Could that be why nearly all civilizations dating back to antiquity distilled intoxicants? Why, when the evening hours close around us and we have no more work to distract our minds, we seek to drown that low whisper that insists so obstinately on meaning—that voice, that ancient and persistent question: *Is this all there is?*

〰

Although I've mellowed considerably from my younger and bourbon-soaked days, when I look back on the decade-and-a-half preceding my father's death, it's sobering to realize just how much I drank. This is not to blame my father unduly for his son's troublesome thirst, but merely to point out that, whatever its origins, intemperance has a way of creeping up on you, of settling into the bosom of the metabolism unfelt. It's easy enough to get deep in the cups, and hangovers, like loneliness, are a condition those of a certain mindset acclimate to. Alcohol as chemotherapy for anxiety, poisoning the patient to cure his ailment—or, as Dorothy Parker famously and impertinently put it, "I'd rather have a bottle in front of me than a frontal lobotomy."

But writers often make light of their drinking, as when Dylan Thomas described an alcoholic as "someone you don't like who drinks as much as you," a joke that, while funny, also reeks of self-protection. Perhaps the biggest pitfall of cracking open a fresh bottle is that it asks no delayed gratification, and writing is nothing if not an extended lesson in exactly that. Instead, the bottle offers a temporary parole from the gulag of consciousness. Drink hard enough for long enough and the imbiber attains the illusion of stepping outside time: the past a fog bereft of meaning; the present a dreary waiting room, like a dentist's office without the *Highlights* magazines and free spools of floss; and the future just a vaguely worrisome abstraction. Seen in this light, *aqua vitae* isn't merely some pithy Latin, but millennia-old black humor.

Properly approached, however, whiskey has an embedded temperance point.

Have one too many and you'll find the taste buds suddenly anesthetized; have another and the tongue thickens to leather; have still another and the head begins to ache; anymore and the head ceases to ache, and there one teeters on a slope at bottom of which can be days of physical and psychic agony.

This stopping point can be ignored, of course—often it is, and gleefully—but it's there. Again, this is purely Epicurean. Flavor can safely be equated with volume. If the spirit can no longer be tasted or scented, or not tasted or scented quite as well, relax and wait for time to recalibrate the senses, to recalibrate *you*. Because when used wisely, single malt is a pleasure that rewards the tempering of wants.

That said, our wants can be tempered too far. My father, for example, was nobody's idea of an epicure. Almost pathologically disdainful of all pleasures, he was more likely to demand to know the price of something (I can still hear his bellowing voice—"How much did that *cost?*"—and see the disabused look on my mother's face in turn) rather than to ask himself whether the thing in question might be of real value. Groceries, for instance. Or clothing. Healthcare. In fact, I'm not certain he believed in the goodness of things at all, let alone a luxury such as single malt. He styled himself an island, and so over time transformed into a walking opinion with nothing of interest to carry an opinion about, a brain wheelbarrowed around by a rusting body, certain that all objects and people in its wake were but mere distractions.

Such a person can seem admirably restrained in their desires, as if they've mastered their needs or conquered the pull of the senses, but in my father's case the situation was otherwise—he was by all accounts a miserable man, even if blind to his own condition. While he had a fraught relationship with his own father, a rural Missouri pig farmer whose crude example drove his son to a life of the mind, and he suffered all the usual disappointments (not the least of which were his sons, for whom the seeds of rebellious self-destruction found fertile soil), I think now his unhappiness owed mostly to simply never having cultivated any real pleasures. This wasn't due to his foregoing pleasure consciously, and certainly not on account of sacrificing his wants to put his family first, but due to a curious skepticism of the simple good. He viewed the world he'd found himself in through an almost comically austere lens. And so he opened himself to the hell of a world that cares nothing for ideologues or their ideals.

The newspaper was his great white whale, his portentous and iron-sided *Gazette,* and it was also a soapbox for the one pseudo-pleasure he did allow himself, which was the joy of denigrating his perceived enemies (liberals, preferably, although a neighbor would do in a pinch). But this was a loveless pleasure, arch and derogatory and underwritten by a cocktail of scorn and ego. What he forgot somewhere along the way, or perhaps simply failed to ever learn, is that we *are* bodies. Thus, denial when his mind began to slip, as he'd watched his mother's mind slip before him. That sole treasured possession and hiding place, slowly losing its words, unable to cobble together the polemics it'd armored itself with for all those years. Money rotting in the bank. Dividends turning over as his house fell down around him. Bulk-ordered memory supplements piling up in a spare room, forgotten. And in the decades before, when his legs and back gave out, his long-neglected body in mutiny for his having failed to ever quite notice it.

Not that I don't sympathize with the urge to live solely in the head. The temptation of a full retreat into one's own thoughts and ideas, the fantasy of the empty room. I understand all of that. We were both readers, he and I, and books are often held up as shields instead of being put to their proper use, as portals.

Much as with overindulgence, austerity reaches a point of no return, where not even beauty or sex or single malt can awaken us to the world our body so briefly passes through. Pleasures must be tended, coddled and indulged like naughty kittens, or else they wither and present a handle we cannot use. Like whiskey in the cask, time reduces us, evaporates us, but it can also deepen and enrich us. A delicate balance, a journey inward and down into the loam of our souls, with the only guides being our senses and the only guideposts those objects we adore.

Khayyám in his *Rubáiyát* bids us drink in response to the pitiless unknowability of our lives and deaths, and in this he's nothing if not Epicurean. To tame a pleasure is to cultivate it, and cultivation is an expression of love. Single malt properly approached is another of these portals. Or at least it can be. And while my father is gone now and my memories of him fade and change, softening in some places and darkening in others, I nonetheless raise a Christmas toast, two fingers of Speyside's finest, if not quite to him then perhaps to some vision I hold of the man I might yet be, which is inevitably a reflection of him. To drink well is to cultivate a value, to reach outward from the confines of the self and risk letting the world in.

A few months before my father's death, I visited home—a home in which I'd never felt comfortable and which as an adult I'd visited as rarely as possible, sometimes not for years at a stretch, and never without a bottle of bourbon in my duffel. My mother had warned me to expect the worst, and yet in his turtling oddity, hollow looks, and groping for language, he and I had gotten along better than we perhaps ever had before. We sat together. Watched a little TV. Lingered over meals. While we hadn't been able to talk much, with the words so went the old animosities. Prior to my father's decline, one of his favorite themes was the certainty of my failure as a writer. His basic premise: I wasn't smart enough to write anything worth reading; I wasn't smarter than my presumed audience, and therefore had no business trying to write. He said this or implied it over and over again, every chance he got, even though he must've known how much it hurt me, and even though he really should've known that, regardless of my intellectual standing as compared to hypothetical others, I definitely *was* smart enough to understand his insults grew out of his own frustrations and embarrassment with the failure of his newspaper. But, if only for one short visit, all of that was gone. I cannot say there was pleasure in this silence, not for either of us, but mercy sometimes comes in strange guise.

On the morning of the last day, I awoke early, washed my face at the sink, and stuffed my dirty clothes into my bourbon-less duffel bag. I recall my father standing a few feet off the porch, wooden-legged, his beard gone to snow. He was dressed strangely, in a castoff jacket of mine from high school and sandals over white athletic socks. He waved as my girlfriend and I backed down the drive in preparation for the long trip north to O'Hare.

Paused in the middle of the street I'd grown up on, in that drifting moment before I shifted the rental from reverse into drive, I said, "That's the last time I'll ever see him."

The certainty I heard in my own voice startled me. But my girlfriend merely watched the old man, whom she'd meet just that once, his lips parted in what might've been a smile but somehow wasn't, not quite, his upraised hand trembling in the brittle air, his eyes the same washed-out blue as the empty December sky.

17
LIFERS AND BAR TIME:
THE STOICS AT LAST CALL

Back when I first began bartending, it'd seemed there could be no worse insult than to be called a "lifer." The slur got tossed around a lot, and always by the young, as to call someone a lifer was to call them a burnout, a last-chancer moldering away in a job more suitable for a college kid. It carried the suggestion of perpetual underachievement, of clinging to youth after the bloom has faded from the rose. Most of all, it implied the lifer might've done something more, something noteworthy, but for whatever reason wouldn't, couldn't, didn't.

I first learned of the term at age twenty-six, working the dayshift back at the Steelhead Bar & Grill. The nightshift bartender was an Irishman named Kevin. He was in his late fifties, wore a grizzled red-gray beard, and habitually memorized a new dirty joke before each shift. But what I remember best about Kevin was his peculiar gait. You couldn't call it a limp, exactly, but there remained something vaguely mechanical in the way he moved.

Without fail, Kevin would clock-in with less than a minute to go before happy hour, buzzed on Starbucks and griping at me for yet again having "set him up to fail" via not cutting enough fruit or chilling enough beer. And in fairness, my restocking duties were of less concern than was Sara, my blue-eyed and magic mushroom-loving waitress girlfriend.

One afternoon after we'd clocked out, she and I decided to stick around for a drink at the bar—at Kevin's bar, that is. Because he took ownership of the oak. The guy was a pro, an old-school bartender with decades of experience, and this entitled him to all the best shifts. This meant he also made a lot of money, or at least a lot compared to the pittance I took home for refilling iced teas and serving salmon burgers to the local old folks.

"So, don't get upset," Sara whispered, "but Kevin asked me to go to Hawai'i with him."

I nearly spat out my bourbon. Sara was twenty-one and gorgeous, whereas Kevin was approaching retirement age and bore a notable resemblance to the title character from the *Leprechaun* franchise of B-grade horror movies. He was also married.

She sipped her beer and squeezed my knee under the bar. "I mean, does he really think I'd . . . just to take a free trip?"

"He must be an optimist," I said.

"No, he's just a lifer," Sara said.

Down the rail, Kevin was busy joking with the Steelhead's clientele, shaking martinis and rattling off those famous off-color jokes. But then another drink chit spat out of the ticker. Kevin snagged it with his free hand, never breaking the rhythm of his shaking or the flow of conversation. After a glance around the bar, however, he frowned.

Then I watched him pop open one of the knee-height fridge doors, lean over, and peer inside. He pushed one arm in to the shoulder, past the frosted martini glasses and bottles of olives and maraschino cherries. But whatever he needed was apparently still out of reach. He stood there a moment, mouth a grim line, and then turned his back on his customers and ratcheted down on one knee. I use the term "ratcheted" because of the herky-jerky way he moved. It wasn't just that Kevin was a little stiff or that getting down on one knee pained him; it were as if his body balked at the prospect, like he was ordering his limbs to perform tasks they'd forgotten how to do, as if the simple motions constituted an intricate physiological riddle.

Once Kevin had finally managed to stick his head in the fridge, he must've confirmed the mystery ingredient wasn't there after all. Was it something I'd forgotten to stock? Then he grabbed the lip of the ice bin and hauled himself back up, cheeks flushed red as his beard. Moments later, having upended a bottle of gin over a mixer pint, he noticed me watching him. "My surgeon said a new hip would have me feeling right as rain," he said, as the liquor roped and plashed, "but surgeons are just like us bartenders—they're only in it for the dough."

Whatever residual annoyance I'd felt over his having propositioned Sara disintegrated in a wash of pity. Bartending every night on an artificial hip—and one that apparently didn't function properly? After we'd tabbed out, I told Sara about Kevin's bum wheel, but she just said that if he was in such bad shape then maybe he should hit on women his own age.

Come the next morning, I shard the story with Abbott. Prior to the Steelhead, he'd managed a busy spot downtown, but the job ended after corporate caught wind of his relationship with a waitress—now his soon-to-be wife. Pushing forty and an industry vet in his own right, Abbott made a point of looking his staff deep in the eye during conversation. He understood how to slow down during the crush and make everyone, from head waiters down to dishwashers, feel noticed and important. He also had a habit of speaking ironically to those with an ironic bent—often at the expense of those without—thereby amusing the former and mystifying the latter. Whenever times got stressful around the Steelhead, I found myself thinking: What Would Abbott Do? I copied his moves and attitude, and usually with good results. We hadn't worked together all that long, but I liked to think we'd become friends.

"I'd noticed he's a little gimpy," Abbott said, "but I didn't know he'd had a hip replacement."

"Can you imagine?"

"He's raking in a grand a week. Sometimes more."

"Sure, but forty hours on your feet with a joint made out of metal?"

Abbott mulled this over, never breaking eye contact with me. "The bills don't stop just because you get older."

Initially, I thought he'd just meant that people have to do whatever is necessary to make ends meet, but maybe it wasn't so simple? Because when I'd told the story of Kevin's bad hip, I'd spoken as if the two of us—Abbott and I—were on different journeys entirely.

Then, seeming lost in thought, Abbott pointed out a small clock beside the taps. "This isn't set for bar time," he said.

I checked my watch. The clock was accurate to the minute.

"Here's a trade secret," he said, and then set the clock ahead fifteen minutes.

"So, bar time is later than regular time?"

Abbott studied the empty restaurant, the idle waitstaff, the bored cooks manning the sauté line. "Stick with this job long enough and you'll find there's less of it come last call," he said.

≈

And stick with it I did. Although, unlike Abbott, when a few years later I left Jackson Hole and returned to Portland to pour craft beer at the Green Dragon, I was still unencumbered by responsibilities. Whereas Abbott had recently become a new father, the timing particularly difficult as his child was born shortly before Rogue Ales bought the Dragon and fired him.

Whenever we met up afterward, he looked evermore haggard and exhausted. His life was coming apart, he said. He was on the cusp of losing his home and, should that happen, his wife had threatened to take their daughter back to the Midwest. An attorney lurked amongst his in-laws. "She and her family are circling the wagons," he said one day. "You wouldn't believe how quick they turned on me."

For a moment I feared Abbott would weep, but instead his soft blue eyes glazed over and he mumbled something odd about living on a houseboat. I understood, at least to some degree, how he felt. Cornered and hounded, he'd aged out of the front lines of the bar game and come up against a wall in his managerial career. Then I recalled that conversation from back at the Steelhead, the one about Kevin's artificial hip. This wasn't pity, though—not the realization that my old mentor was a lifer, too—but something more akin to fear. Because I was feeling older, as well. I still wasn't quite thirty at that point, which is certainly young, and yet the dozen or so years between Abbott and I felt like far less. And if the difference between us wasn't so great, what of Kevin?

The shadow beneath all such anxiety is, of course, mortality. And when we consider this particular topic—or when this particular topic simply won't allow us to continue *not* considering it—we find our culture offers little guidance. This is because we've relegated the reality of the single most human thing about us, which is our awareness of the short time in which we get to *be* human, to taboo. As James Baldwin writes, the root of our trouble is that we'll gladly sacrifice life's beauty and imprison our minds, "in order to deny the fact of death, the only fact we have." Blame notions of the afterlife or blame a culture that prioritizes the individual to the point that individuals can no longer imagine a universe without them in it or blame youth-obsessed media or a thousand other things. Regardless, the result looks not unlike a massive cult of death-deniers. And while this is certainly understandable, it results in us failing in the most manifestly basic of ways to understand ourselves.

Fortunately, however, wise people have put their minds to this topic and offered up a host of practical advice—you just have to go back a couple millennia.

The ancient Stoics (Baldwin likely would've counted as one, had he been around back then) tackled mortality head-on and without apology. Take Seneca, who was both an influence on Montaigne as well as tutor to the young Nero—although the pupil later instructed the master to commit suicide. Not that Seneca wasn't prepared. In one of his surviving writings, he compares life to a lamp. Is a lamp, he asks, any worse off after it's extinguished than before it was lit? If not, what is there for us at either end but a deep tranquility? So, when Seneca crawled into a bath to oblige his emperor, he died according to the very principles he'd taught.

Along with the Epicureans and the Cynics before them, the Stoics more or less dismissed questions of the afterlife. Their materialism would largely disappear by the third century, overshadowed by the new Christianity, and they wouldn't be heard from again until the Renaissance. But the Stoics remain instructive, insofar as they outline how an individual might go about approaching life when that life feels utterly uncertain and often meaningless. Death is a reminder of how best to live, but nothing to truly be feared. Why chase after money or praise or fame, when soon enough nobody will be around to remember anyway? Loss isn't loss but change, and change is inevitable. And the immensity of time: that's our proper lens, our perspective. Happiness in such a philosophy isn't a thing to be gotten—not a *having*—but a state of being predicated upon recognition and acceptance of the simplest of realism.

One drizzly night a few months before the Rogue buyout and that worrisome conversation with Abbott, I gave Gamby a ride home after we'd closed up shop. Lookswise, Gamby fell somewhere between Santa Claus and a Hell's Angel. His nickname owed to King Gambrinus, the mythic beer patron of Belgium, a jolly and hirsute fellow who's usually depicted with a tankard of ale raised to his mouth. Like the King, Gamby was tall and keg-bellied, and between the two of us my little Honda was riding the rims.

Curbside at his place, he lingered as if something were on his mind. Finally, he asked whether I liked tending bar. I didn't want to sugarcoat my true feelings, but I also didn't want to seem unappreciative of the job I'd been given. "Yeah, I like it well enough."

He nudged me with an elbow the size of a cue ball. "You sure about that, man?"

Bartender burnout is a common affliction, and mine was apparently showing. "Well, my feet didn't hurt this much a few years ago. That's for sure."

"Wait until you're forty. My dogs bark every night. I gotta soak 'em in Epsom salts."

But when I asked Gamby if *he* still liked tending bar, he smiled faintly before admitting to having tried pretty much every job there was, from cooking to real estate. Blue-collar, white-collar, no collar. But nothing ever quite stuck. When he hauled himself up from the passenger seat, the suspension groaned and the chassis raised two inches. "So, I keep coming back to bartending," he said. "Pay's good and the customers are nice"—his brow wrinkled like an accordion—"most of the time."

Before heading inside, Gamby lowered his face to the window. His bearded jaws glistened with rainwater. "Think about it this way," he said. "Maybe bartending is a job for people who for whatever reason fail at everything else."

I laughed—scoffed, really. "Then you're saying we're *failures?*"

"No, man." He straightened up and patted the Honda's roof. "I'm saying we're bartenders."

That conversation has stuck with me over the years, and lately it's come to seem telling. A calling for those for whom the world is otherwise mysteriously lacking? A refusal to allow common sentiment to determine your worth, or how you feel about your own peculiar lot in life?

What simple but extraordinary statements—and Stoic ones at that.

Epictetus, who began life as a Roman slave, believed humanity was troubled by a tendency to worry incessantly over a mortality that cannot be avoided, while failing to worry sufficiently about what can be controlled, and to thereby confuse our desires and aversions such that we bungle the key to contentment, which he phrases in his *Discourses* as, "whether you do not fail to get what you wish, or do not fall into what you do not wish." While the negative phrasing makes for some confusion, the key word is *wish.* The point is not achievement in the traditional sense, which inevitably implies the perceptions of others, but serenity, which requires we observe and understand what is actually meaningful—to us. Failure in such a conception doesn't lie in the job itself or even how it's performed, but in how we conceive or fail to conceive of it.

Epictetus's writings had a profound effect on Thomas Jefferson, in particular in dealing with his encroaching mortality, a topic Jefferson never shied away from. But a more contemporary admirer was his fellow Stoic, the Roman emperor Marcus Aurelius, who writes in his *Meditations* that we should remember things do not and cannot touch our souls, despite how they seem to, as things are external and fixed—"but our perturbations," he notes, "come only from the opinion which is within." The emperor was no Pollyanna, though. The bulk of his writings were composed amidst an extended and bloody campaign against the neighboring barbarians, and his thinking reflects that. He believes we should see our lives as of little value, considering how many of us there are, have been, and will be, and how feeble and brief is our time. Control is an illusion, as is the sense that we, out of all the billions, are uniquely situated.

But the trouble with philosophy is actually putting it into practice, a difficulty Jefferson noted when he criticized the Stoics for the "hypocrisy and grimace" by which they sought to rationalize away the very real pain of being human. And when it comes to that sort of pain, what was true in the Classical Era and in early America remains just as true now, and one morning maybe four months after Abbot told me of his disintegrating home life, he called in a bad state.

"I need a loan," he said, and I could hear the distress and shame in his voice. While it wasn't a huge amount he asked for, it wasn't exactly a small amount, either. But because he was my friend, and because he'd given me a job—and, most of all, because of that awful tremor in his voice—I didn't hesitate to cut the check. I did wonder if I were making a mistake, though. Not as to whether I'd be paid back, but as to what use he might put the funds.

I heard from him only a few more times after that, ever more anxious, ever grayer, until one morning he phoned at dawn. I'd closed the bar the night before and was still asleep. The message he left was brief, just his soft and familiar voice asking me to please call back when I awoke. But when I finally did, no answer. And none the next day, nor the day after that. In the weeks to come, I learned that none of our mutual friends had heard from him, either, including one guy who'd also loaned some money. Soon thereafter, Abbott's phone went dead.

~

Four years later, having taken Abbott's long-ago advice and washed up in Hawai'i, I couldn't help but wonder if Lana'i might not be the very same island Kevin had hoped to take Sara to for that romantic getaway. And while my job with the Four Seasons and Nobu was a good one, I was nonetheless apprehensive. Another bar gig? My thirty-fourth birthday was right around the bend. Thirty-four seemed significant in a way thirty-three somehow hadn't. It wasn't that I'd managed to outlive the savior, and it wasn't that the following birthday would set me rolling on the downslope to forty. Maybe it was because the multiplication of my age by three (echoes of the Trinity despite my agnosticism?) would now break the three-digit barrier and thus no longer result in an integer in which I might still feasibly be alive? Whatever the case, it was the first time I'd seen myself as anything less than completely *young*. Ugly possibilities intruded upon my beachy vibes. A few decades on, was it my fate to be limping around behind some tiki bar and drooling over twentysomething waitresses who only returned my awkward middle-aged flirtations so that I'd continue surreptitiously dosing their Sprites with vodka?

So, yes, the long-overdue question finally had to be asked: was I really a *lifer?*

I wasn't alone, though, as virtually everyone on Lana'i was an industry lifer, considering there were few other jobs that paid a living wage. Still, the fear I'd begun to sense back at the Green Dragon had now deepened into full-blown dread. Here I was in paradise, living out the mainlander's fantasy of escaping to the exotic, a guy who rolled into work tanned and cologned in saltwater and suntan oil from a day at the beach—and yet I couldn't shake the creeping empty. Like a tropical mold, my anxiety grew with the passing months. I pumped weights at the gym until my shoulders threatened to split the seams of my ninja-black uniform shirts, endlessly walked the island's quiet and narrow streets, took sketchings of the old-time pre-World War II feel of the place, debated creationism with the Jehovah's Witnesses, ate fresh poke bowls from the local shops, and, of course, I wrote. I even began dragging my laptop down to the beach, sitting with my back against a palm tree and dreaming up a story about a floundering rural Illinois car lot as the sun glinted off the sea and fresh-caught opakapaka browned on the grills.

On the surface at least, my situation seemed fine—more than fine. My finances were in as much order as my finances ever are, my coworkers were kind and amusing people, and the island was a perpetual and buttery seventy-eight degrees, a place tourists forked over upwards of a thousand dollars nightly to visit. Nonetheless, despite the island's aloha spirit and the waves breaking on the golden crescent of Hulopo'e Bay and the perfume of orchids and plumeria on the breeze—despite how at dusk the resort came ablaze with torches and an islander in a sarong sounded a conch from the deck and the ukulele musician strummed those haunting covers of Israel Kamakawiwo'ole—despite the seeming tranquility of such a life, I was miserable.

Above all, the *Meditations* insist we remember our brevity, and this I was not doing, at least not in any useful way. Instead, I was thinking of what'd come before and what might come next: what I hadn't yet done, and still might yet do, which is another way of saying I was failing to see time not as an endless resource, the way a kid sees it, but as what it truly is: the opportunity for being ticking away in the here and now.

The Stoics offer no easy answers here, though. Due to their ambivalence about the afterlife, they lacked a convenient means to rectify the passage of time. All they felt sure of was that mortality weighted the ledger of a life. Our unique foreknowledge, while distressing, provides context, and the wisest of teachers, the greatest of generals, the richest and the most revered of citizens—and, to reach our inevitable conclusion, the most melancholy of Pacific isle bartenders— all end up the same way: as "Smoke and ash and a tale, or not even a tale."

One slow night at work, I noticed the bar's espresso machine had a small clock with glowing green numerals. Four Seasons and Nobu aren't the sort of establishments where drunk customers get herded out at last call, so setting the clocks ahead to bar time wasn't really necessary. Still, I found myself remembering Abbott, who'd first introduced me to the concept. I wondered what'd become of him, where he'd gone, what he still believed in. Finally, I decided to reset the clock after all, except while punching the buttons I set it backward fifteen minutes: then fifteen more: then an hour: then two.

≈

A few years down the line, during the period when I tended bar at that decaying and gothic Italian restaurant north of Seattle, I got to feeling nostalgic one day and headed down I-5 to Portland. At one of the taphouses I visited there, I spied a familiar face—Gamby. He was still a big dude, but he'd slimmed down considerably. His hair was thinner and he moved a little slower. Otherwise, he seemed like the same easygoing guy. We chatted about what'd become of everyone from the Green Dragon, this person landed here, this person landed there, and I couldn't resist asking if he'd heard tell of Abbott.

Gamby leaned over the bar on his big elbows and spoke quietly. "He's still around somewhere. Or at least he was. I bumped into him at a festival once, out east of the mountains."

"Did he seem okay?"

"No, man. I can't say that he did."

Then I asked if he knew what'd become of Abbott's family.

As if he'd readied himself for this very question, Gamby took a deep breath and measured his words. I recalled that rain-smeared night years before when he'd asked if I liked tending bar. I'd fessed up to certain reservations then, and now Gamby didn't sugarcoat things either. "Some guys just get overwhelmed," he said. "Like the walls are closing in, like there's a wolf inside your chest trying to chew its way out. Haven't you ever felt that way?"

When I couldn't find any useful words and merely looked down into my pint, he left to tend his other customers. The news hadn't come as a surprise, necessarily, but I'd hoped things had turned out differently. Abbott had been a mentor of sorts, after all, an older male presence I'd needed at a certain point—a

Coughlin to my second-rate Tom Cruise. He was also a lifer, though. But by the time I'd finished that pint, it struck me that what had at first seemed pitiful and sad, then later distressing and fearful, was actually just another inevitability, like smoke and ash.

～

The Stoics were refreshingly forthright in their belief that our lives are but flickers of light between vast gulfs of nothingness. It's the soberest of realism. *Memento mori* and the ticking clock. The grinning skull and the hourglass. It's the awakening of adolescence and the anxiety of middle-age and the resignation at day's end. Because when looked at by the numbers, we do seem more than a little transitory. Think of the Copernican revolution and heliocentricity (which, much as with atoms, the Classical Greeks intuited but had no means of proving), then imagine one of those first photographs of Earth as seen from space, and then try to imagine the Stoics, nearly two millennia before, abstracting and hypothesizing and dollying their perspective back nearly that far, doing their best to assess their place in the universe honestly and rationally. From such a vantage, human lives do all seem more or less the same, and short. So, perhaps the Stoics are right, and despite our pretensions of meaning we're actually just little blades of grass that sprout up for a few days before the Great Lawnmower of Time comes along and chops us down.

This isn't to marginalize our species, though, nor to imply we shouldn't care deeply about ourselves and our fellow creatures, but to suggest we should try not to lose perspective and let the inevitable pains and disappointments take on greater importance than they actually warrant. Maybe our inability to keep this perspective, a cultural if not even genetic vanity and myopia, is to blame for a world promised that bears so little resemblance to the world bequeathed?

Whatever the case, Stoic ideas have survived these two millennia, and so I sit at my writing desk—a desk in a house situated just outside of Portland, no less, as I eventually met a lovely young woman who brought my travels full circle—and take a crack at them now. To the left of my notebook stands a pile of ungraded student essays ringed in coffee stains, as lately I've been spending my days teaching writing courses at a nearby community college. Teaching is considerably easier on the knees, of course, and yet to the right of those essays sits a freshly printed résumé. But unlike that résumé I toted into the Steelhead fifteen years ago, this one is no fabrication; it lists the string of bars I spent my youth tending—the bars described in this book, the ones full of good and generous people and problem drinkers, of struggling artists and dreamers, of misfits and exiles. The itch to be behind the oak has never quite gone away, I guess. Maybe it never will? And maybe that's okay.

Book Two of *Meditations* begins with the advice to awaken each day knowing full well you'll encounter people who are ungrateful, deceitful, antisocial, and so on, but that these flaws shouldn't anger us or drag us down because we're all cut from the same cloth, and we need to cooperate as best we can while we can. Later, in Book Four, the emperor quotes his old mentor Epictetus, who says a person is just a little soul bearing around a corpse. And if that's not good advice for a bartender—and for a teacher—then I don't know what philosophy to embrace.

Then again, it's also possible Abbott and Gamby were right: maybe there really is less time come last call, and perhaps a bartender really is just a person who for whatever reason fails at everything else. Maybe, like Jefferson believed, Stoicism is a useful ethical framework, but to pretend philosophy can provide any real balm for the darker aspects of the human condition is mere self-delusion. But whatever its shortcomings, Stoicism is a way of remembering that we're all of us lifers, and that we're all living on bar time. So, if Seneca was correct and our lives are like lamps, then in these brief intervals when our wicks are actually lit, we'd best not squander the light with constant worry over the tasks required of us to keep body and soul together.

That said, even now I can feel a pinch deep in my left hip. When I stand or walk, it settles into a dullish ache that worsens with the passing hours. It's flared up only recently, as if to herald the coming of yet another birthday. I assume this pain will fade and pass. That it's something that will heal—an injury, not a life sentence. But I don't know this for certain any more than I know I'll rise from bed tomorrow for certain. It's the decay and strife yet to come, the deepening lines on a face reflected in a darkened windowpane, the aching back, the gray molar. Regardless, I can put on a stoic face and ignore this pain in my hip for the time being. Stretch to keep limber, pop a few ibuprofen in the morning and drink a few cold beers come dusk. But it'd be disingenuous of me to pretend I don't also sometimes grimace and wonder: to what end?

≈

One possible answer came just recently, when that long-suffering novel—the one about the car salesmen in rural Illinois—found an indie publisher willing to give it a chance. Not much glory will come of it, in all likelihood, and even less money, but I finished the book. It's done and it's good (I hope), and soon enough it'll be out in the world where creative things belong.

This in tandem with a second book—a nonfiction tour of Pacific Northwest beer country with Robert Burton (*The Anatomy of Melancholy*) as a guide—leaves me in the curious-if-commonplace position of feeling somewhat validated in my writerly aspirations, yet still needing to work various non-writing gigs to support my writing habit. It may sound selfish to admit, but I do wish my father were still around to see my books in print. I doubt he'd have actually liked them very much, and I don't believe they'd have ultimately changed his mind about his youngest son's inevitable literary failure (nothing short of a million dollar advance could've done that), but I like to think some deeply buried and never-spoken part of him might have been grudgingly impressed. If only by my grit and patience.

But that's not the way the cookie crumbled, and as anybody who's ever honestly tried to create something—a book, an identity—will attest, the rewards, such as they are, can only ever really be internal. To seek outside validation from anyone or anything, be it a parent or an entire society, is to court misery, and the work must be its own reward, the process the reason, the end result, if an end can ever really be reached, a sort of Zen missive offered up to the wind and time.

Bartending and booze may or may not have actually helped me become a writer—the archetypal myth of drunken inspiration, à la Tennessee Williams or William Faulkner, Jean Rhys or Lucia Berlin or any other drinker who's ever scribbled a line, is just that: a myth—but the job and the lifestyle did allow me to support myself while exploring the American West, introduced me to some unforgettable characters, and left me with a few choice stories. Like the Jack London of *John Barleycorn*, it's fair to say I have a love-hate relationship with bars and drinking—but, honestly, having come to the other side of it in one piece, it's mostly love. Because while my life behind bars hasn't always been easy or pleasant, the bar provided me something of real value, both as a writer and as a person: a thorough grounding in the tortoise-like and unglamorous reality of self-reinvention. Change of any meaningful sort is grueling. Hence, faith is required, secular or otherwise and the more irrationally dogmatic the better. Emerson, whose essays I still return to, believed our power as individuals resides in transformation, that we are at our best in a state of flux, and that our deepest identity is metamorphosis: that "the soul *becomes*."

Admittedly, listening to Emerson can be trouble. But I suspect he's onto something.

Distillation is the extraction and purification of the essential, which is what I've tried to do here: distill my life in bars. It's become fashionable of late to dismiss memoir and other forms of personal storytelling as solipsism or navel-gazing, but it's also been said that those who write about themselves aren't so much recalling the past as trying to make sense of it—consciousness wresting memory—and I believe that's true, much as I believe each person's experience, no matter how humble, carries universal meaning.

But maybe not. Maybe that's wishful thinking and the real truth is that our work, no matter how dear to us, is ultimately just cosmic trivia, the identity forged from that work of little significance, lessons illusory, the search for meaning a pathetic mewl into the vacuum.

Faced with such possibilities, one course alone seems reasonable—find a good friend and then find a good bar. A bar where nicks and dings anoint elbow-polished wood, and the air is rich with malted barley. A bar where music hums soft as the pool table's brushed felt run, taps shine like votary candles, and a dram glows as if imbued with all the luster of fading day. Now open a tab, cloister down into a booth, and amidst the rye and peat, the oak and sour mash, the anecdotes and confession, strive for that finest of all human connections: the soul-melding oneness of a sympathetic buzz. Failing that, just stay for a while. Relax. Reflect. Notice the tastes. The smells. The delicacy of the Brussels lace, that latticework of dying foam, as it notches down the pint like gossamer cobwebs, like the hours themselves, sip by precious sip.

ACKNOWLEDGMENTS

Grateful acknowledgment is made to the editors of the various literary magazines whose time and attention helped improve these essays prior to their collection as a book, and to the publications listed below, in which some of these essays appeared in slightly different form. Also, special thanks to Chris Schacht, Rus Bradburd, Andrew Milward and Gina Colantino. And thank you to everyone at Bauhan Publishing: Sarah Bauhan, Mary Ann Faughnan, Henry James, and Lexi Palmer.

"Aqua Vitae" *Water~Stone Review*. Vol. 23, 2020. Print.

"Beer Quarters" *Oxford Magazine*. 2020. Web.

"Dark Sunglasses" *Green Briar Review*. Spring 2019. Web.

"Dramming with Frank O'Brien" *Ponder Review*. Spring 2019. Print.

"Happy Hour in an Italian Restaurant" *Reed Magazine*. Issue 153, Spring 2020. Print.

"Hodads in Wonderland" *Post Road Magazine*. Issue 38, 2020–2021. Print.

"In Praise of Four Loko: Moonlighting in the Land of Enchantment" *The Doctor T. J. Eckleburg Review*. Issue 21, Spring 2020. Print.

"Sgailc: The Art of Making Poisons Pleasant" *Gold Man Review*. November 2019. Print.

"Terroir" *The Missouri Review*. Vol. 43:4, Winter 2020. Print.

"The Machine in Our Pocket: Drinking Alone in iPhone World" *The Briar Cliff Review*. 2020. Print.

"Whiskey Boys" *River Teeth: A Journal of Nonfiction Narrative*. Vol. 21 no. 2, Spring 2020. Print.